IMAGES
of America

THE SEA RANCH

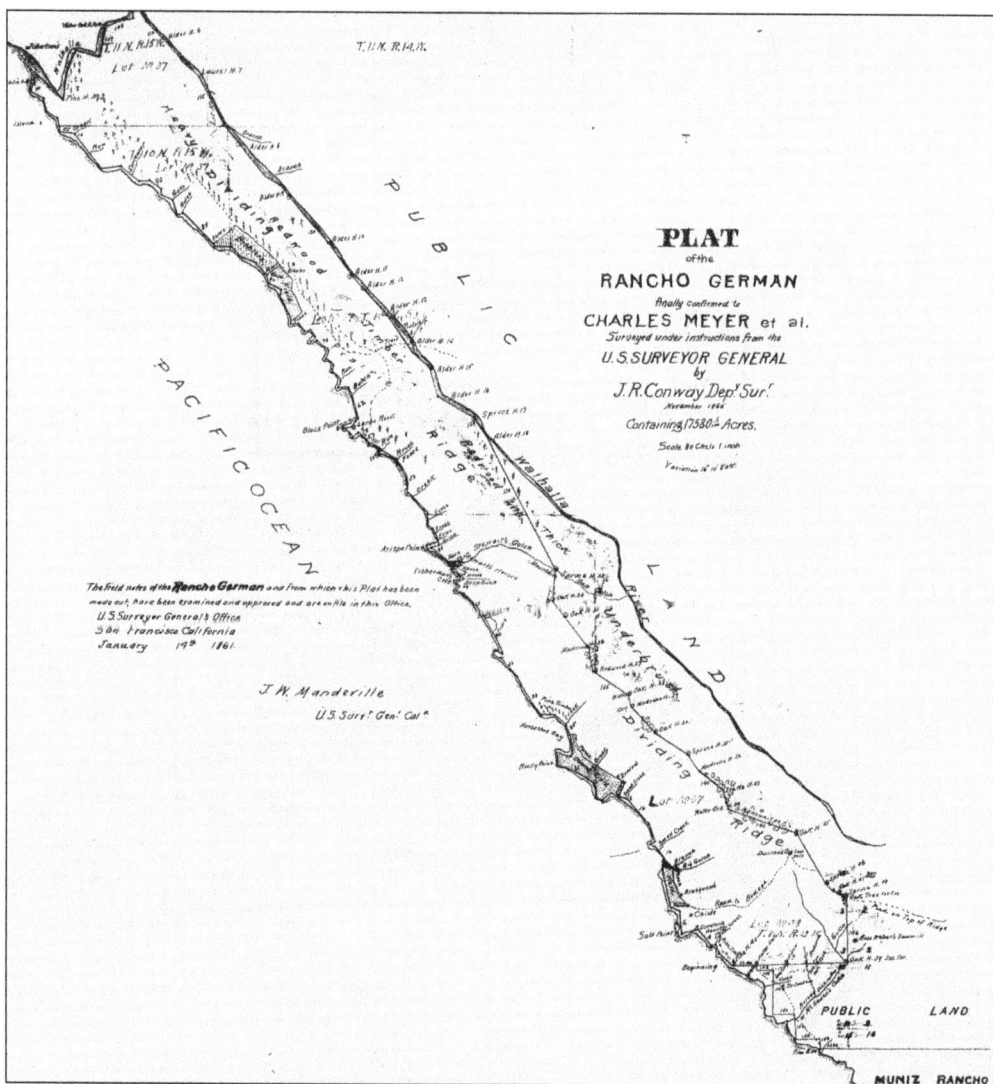

PLAT
of the
RANCHO GERMAN
finally confirmed to
CHARLES MEYER et al.
Surveyed under instructions from the
U.S. SURVEYOR GENERAL
by
J.R. Conway Dep.' Sur.'
November 1860
Containing 17580½ Acres.
Scale 80 Chains 1 inch
Variation 16° 15' East.

The field notes of the *Rancho German* and from which this Plat has been
made out, have been examined and approved and are on file in this Office.
U.S. Surveyor General's Office
San Francisco California
January 19th 1861.

J.W. Manderville
U.S. Surr.' Gen.' Cal.°

The U.S. government required owners of Mexican land grants to present their titles to the federal courts to have the grants confirmed by U.S. courts. Confirmation proceedings took place throughout the 1850s. Many owners could not afford the legal fees, delays, and uncertainties the process required, so they sold or abandoned their claim. The German Rancho was confirmed in 1852 and again in 1855. The land was surveyed by the U.S. Surveyor General to determine its exact boundaries, and the plat map was produced in 1861. The government then offered for public sale the land outside the boundaries. (Courtesy of U.S. Bureau of Land Management.)

ON THE COVER: Rocks that spread out below the headlands permit fishermen to escape the wind, which whips across the west meadows. Russ Ohlson was fishing on the rocks below Del Mar Landing when this photograph was taken in the late 1940s. The building seen above, on the bluff, was the machine shop for the Del Mar Mill, which burned in 1910. The machine shop was the last remaining building of a group of mill structures, originally constructed by brothers William and George Bender in 1898. (Courtesy of the Ohlson family.)

IMAGES
of America

THE SEA RANCH

Susan M. Clark

ARCADIA
PUBLISHING

Published by Arcadia Publishing
Charleston, South Carolina

Library of Congress Control Number: 2008933027

For all general information contact Arcadia Publishing at:
Telephone 843-853-2070
Fax 843-853-0044
E-mail sales@arcadiapublishing.com
For customer service and orders:
Toll-Free 1-888-313-2665

Visit us on the Internet at www.arcadiapublishing.com

To Tom Cochrane, who for 20 years has nudged me back out onto
The Sea Ranch landscape whenever I get too focused on research and
paperwork. He looks at the geology and links it together with historic use
of the property. Our explorations never fail to reignite my enthusiasm.

CONTENTS

ACKNOWLEDGMENTS

Since I first purchased property on The Sea Ranch in 1976, I have wondered and mused about the daily lives of the early settlers on this windswept remote coast. I have carried maps—some hand-drawn, others unrecorded and obscure—as I have explored the landscape for remnants of early buildings and artifacts. Research materials were scarce, and the best sources were old-timers and their descendants. Fortunately, I had the foresight to audio tape dozens of their interviews. Much of the material comes from three decades of interviews as well as searching in the landscape, collecting old photographs, and documenting what traces remain.

Many of my sources are now gone, and my collection contains some of the only photographs and primary records still in existence. I am grateful to Tom Cochrane who helped me select the information and the photographs to include in this book. This is an attempt to share and preserve some of this data. I hope it will give readers a sense of the past and a connection to the land that otherwise might not be noticed or appreciated.

Individuals with intimate knowledge of the coast and others who have had a passion for history have shared their personal experiences and photographs with me. Some like Harold Christensen, Bus Richardson, Bernard Parks, Alice Fiscus, Ed Ohlson, and Richard Tooker have passed on. Others like Janann Strand, Pat (Ohlson) Ashurst, and the Richardson family still share my passion for the history of The Sea Ranch and continue to contribute to coastal history.

Many of the photographs and maps come from my personal collections. Photographer Bob Lee shared several of his images of the early history of the coast. The Richardson family generously provided many of the images in chapters three and four. Seth Adams, historian of Walter Frick's activities in the Mount Diablo area, gave me the wonderful gift of professionally scanned images from the Frick family photo albums. The Ohlson family photographs in chapter seven were provided by the Ohlson family. Original photographs of the World War II military camp were given to me many years ago by Roy Disotelle. I wish to express my gratitude to each of these people.

INTRODUCTION

The northern Sonoma coast was one of the stops on the seasonal route the Pomo Indians made from their inland villages in search of food. They gathered food from the sea, which they either dried or ate fresh. The Pomo Indians left few artifacts, except for occasional arrowheads, mortar and pestles, and shell middens, attesting the purposes of their visits.

Explorers from several countries visited the coast prior to 1800, but none had established any permanent settlement. The Spanish, and later the Mexicans, had come up from the south and settled in California as far north as San Francisco. In 1812, when the Russians moved down from Alaska and established a fur-trading colony on the Sonoma coast, the Spanish pushed up into Sonoma County to block the Russians from further southern expansion. During the early 1800s, the Russians hunted sea otter from the Ross settlement until the otter population was decimated. By 1841, with the sea otter gone, the colonists were ready to get what money they could for the improvements they were leaving behind at Ross and sail back to their native county. John Sutter, of Sutter's Fort fame, purchased the Russians' cattle, supplies, and buildings, but what the purchase did not include was the land.

John Sutter encouraged other Germans to possibly establish a German colony in Northern California. Other European countries had foreign colonies at the time—but not Germany. Although many German families immigrated to the United States in the late 19th century, the early Germans settlers in this area were single, young men.

In 1846, Ernest Rufus, a naturalized Mexican citizen, received from the Mexican government a 17,580-acre land grant, which stretched south from the Gualala River to Ocean Cove. Since Mexican law mandated that grantees make improvements on the land, Rufus sent German immigrant Frederick Hugal to the property, which was called Rancho de Hermann, or simply the German Rancho, a year earlier. Hugal built a cabin and planted an orchard and vegetables on the hill above the present Equestrian Center and constructed a warehouse near the bluff at the north end of Unit 36. Hugal developed a large livestock operation, which passed through ownership of several other Germans before coming to rest in the hands of William Bihler in the 1850s. Bihler turned over management of the ranch to his nephews Chris Stengel and Adam Knipp by 1860. Stengel and Knipp lived on the hill near Hugal's cabin and engaged in stock raising, logging, and shipping for the next 40 years. They referred to their property as the Gualala, or Walhhala, Ranch.

Logging and milling became significant activities on the Knipp Stengel Ranch during the last half of the 19th century. In 1897–1898, brothers William and George Bender constructed a mill and landing a few miles north of Stengel's house and purchased the entire 5,000-acre ranch when Stengel and Knipp retired and sold out in 1904. The mill and landing brought workers to the nearby area, and the settlement they formed took on the name Rancho Del Mar, or the Del Mar Ranch, which we know today as The Sea Ranch. When the Del Mar Mill burned in 1910, the residents dispersed and some headed to mills in Mendocino County, east to farms in Annapolis, or south to Stewarts Point, where mills were still in operation.

Transportation to this remote corner of Sonoma County has always been difficult. There was no continuous road along the coast from Jenner until the 1920s. Prior to that time, travelers came from what is now Highway 116 and had to pass through Cazadero before dropping down to the coast around Fort Ross. They then had to endure travel on a muddy, unpaved road crossed by several gates, which were intended to restrain livestock from wandering and to identify property boundaries.

The most common way for passengers and cargo to arrive and depart from the area was by ship. Schooners usually arrived at Point Arena or Bourne's Landing, just north of Gualala. In the late 1870s, landings were constructed at Stewarts Point and at Black Point, and the lumber trade increased dramatically. Ships would anchor in coves where passengers or freight would be transported to shore by way of a cable or small rowboat, and lumber ready for shipping would arrive on a chute from the bluff above. Two additional landings, Tongue's Landing and Del Mar Landing, were constructed near the north end of the ranch.

In the late 1870s, H. A. Richardson and his wife, Althea, arrived at Stewarts Point and within a couple of years took over the property, including the store. They and their descendants have operated a general merchandise store ever since that time. German ranchers, lumbermen, early settlers, and today's Sea Ranchers have all sought supplies from the Richardsons at Stewarts Point. They have operated a shipping port, railroad, lumber mills, and a livestock operation along with the general merchandise store. Almost every traveler who has ever arrived at Sea Ranch has made a stop at Stewarts Point on the way north.

Following the retirement of Chris Stengel and Adam Knipp in 1904 and the burning of the Del Mar Mill in 1910, a colony of several hundred Baptist-Russian immigrants purchased the ranch. They successfully planted fruits and vegetables until they lost the property to foreclosure. The land was acquired by a Bay Area businessman named Walter P. Frick who introduced raising sheep and had the hedgerows planted. Frick hired a foreman to handle the day-to-day ranching operations while he and his family continued to reside in the Bay Area and use the property as a vacation retreat. Frick died in the late 1930s, and his ranch was auctioned for nonpayment of back taxes in 1941.

Ed, Ches, Ernie, and Elmer Ohlson, sheep raisers from Annapolis, were the only interested people who showed up the day Frick's Del Mar Ranch was auctioned on the steps of the Contra Costa County courthouse. Following their purchase, Ed and his wife and children and Ches moved into the house between the coast road and Del Mar Landing, which had been occupied by the Bender Brothers Mill foreman and later used by the Frick family. Elmer Ohlson took over a small house that had originally been built for Frick's foreman, which stood to the south of the Knipp Stengel Barn below the present eucalyptus crown. The Ohlson family, who owned the property from 1941 to 1965, was the first family to live and work on Sea Ranch for more than just a few years.

Oceanic Properties, Inc., a subsidiary of Castle and Cooke of Hawaii, purchased the 5,000-acre Ohlson ranch with plans to develop the property into a second-home community of 5,000 houses. A five-year-long battle with the California Coastal Commission, from 1976 to 1981, resulted in the reduction of the number of parcels to 2,329. By the mid-1990s, the developer had sold or turned over all the properties to other entities, individuals, or the local homeowners' association. By 2009, over 1,765 houses had been constructed on the Sea Ranch. Development from its inception in 1965 has attempted to preserve the wild and scenic coastline and hide or blend buildings into the environment.

The Sea Ranch was not simply an "instant community" that was developed and sprang up in the mid-1960s. As the Del Mar Ranch, it had experienced a rich history of ranching, logging, shipping, and even World War II military activities.

One

NINETEENTH-CENTURY CATTLE RANCH

1845–1904

The diseño was an 1845 sketch map of the coastal land that was bound by the Gualala River on the north and east and extended southward to include five Spanish leagues. The southern boundary, which was later contested, was identified as Arroyo Dichcalha. William Benitz of Fort Ross drew the diseño from memory after he and fellow German immigrant Ernest Rufus visited the property. Rufus submitted the map to Gov. Pio Pico as part of his application for the German Rancho. His request to Pio Pico stated that he owned a considerable amount of stock, cattle, and horses and needed a tract of land to build a house and keep his livestock. Rufus received a provisional grant in 1845, which was finalized in April 1846 after he reported that he had made improvements on the property. The improvements were made by German immigrant Frederick Hugal, who built a house, warehouse, and gristmill and planted an orchard. The 1860 official survey of the German Rancho determined that the southern boundary was just north of today's Ocean Cove.

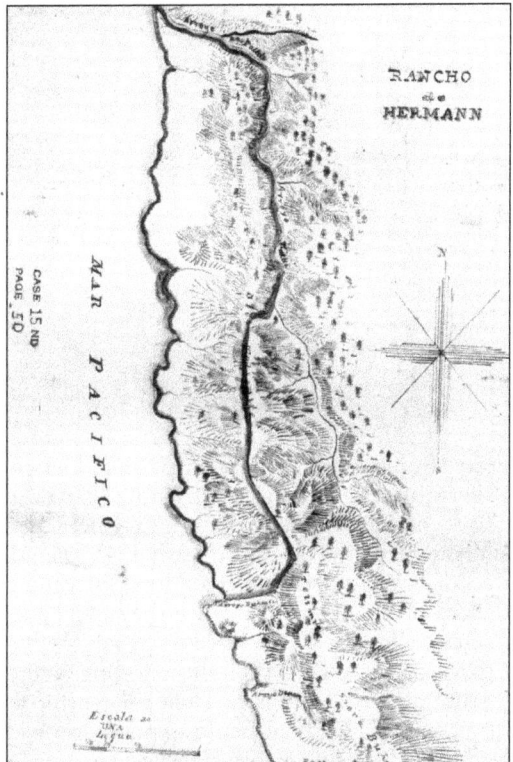

Ernest Rufus arrived in California from Germany in 1838. He earned Mexican citizenship in 1844 for his military service of training Native American soldiers at Sutter's Fort. As a naturalized citizen, he was eligible to apply for a land grant from the government. Rufus was visiting with William Benitz at Fort Ross in early 1845 when the two decided to apply for a five Spanish league tract of land just to the north of Ross. They intended that they would occupy the Ross lands and the property to the north, which they could operate as one large cattle ranch. They agreed that Benitz would draw the required diseño and Rufus would take it first to the Alcalde in Sonoma for a provisional grant and then the following year to Los Angeles and submit it as part of his request for the grant to be finalized. Their partnership fell apart when Rufus took title to the land in his name only and, without Benitz's knowledge, sold off sections of the property to fellow Germans Frederick Hugal and Henry Hageler.

10

Christian Stengel

By 1857, the northern 4,819 acres of the German Rancho were in the hands of William Bihler, a German immigrant who came to California from Baltimore in 1849. Bihler built a house on the same hill where Hugal built his cabin in 1845. At about the same time, Bihler also acquired a large tract on the Huichica Rancho where he resided the rest of his life. To oversee his ranches, Bihler sent to Baltimore for four of his nephews: 21-year-old Adam Knipp, 19-year-old Jacob Stengel, 17-year-old Christian Stengel, and 17-year-old Jacob Grengnagel. The two Jacobs were assigned to Bihler's Huichica property and Chris Stengel and Adam Knipp to the German Rancho. By 1861, Knipp and Stengel were raising cattle, donkeys, horses, and hogs. Over the next 40 years, Knipp and Stengel gradually acquired Bihler's 4,819 acres, which they developed into a large stock-raising ranch that provided a ton of beef each week to the Gualala Mill. Neither man ever married or had a family, so in 1903, when they retired, the entire property was sold to William and George Bender, who transferred it to the Bender Mill and Lumber Company the following year.

Theses sketches, drawn about 1880 by Charles W. Nystrom, are the earliest known images of Sea Ranch. Born in New Jersey in 1830, Charles W. Nystrom was attracted to California in 1852 by the stories of the Gold Rush. By the 1880s, he was in the lumber industry in northern Sonoma and Mendocino Counties. The 1880 census lists him as a 50-year-old unmarried bookkeeper for a logging company. He was living with nine other men, eight of whom were Chinese laborers. Eight of his pencil drawings are in the Bancroft Library in Berkeley. On the above sketch, Nystrom drew the coastline stretching southward from Black Point. The exact location of the sketch is easily identifiable today. The sketch below shows horses grazing on the bluff and the coastline from Black Point to Gualala. Nystrom died in October 1882 and is buried at Stewarts Point.

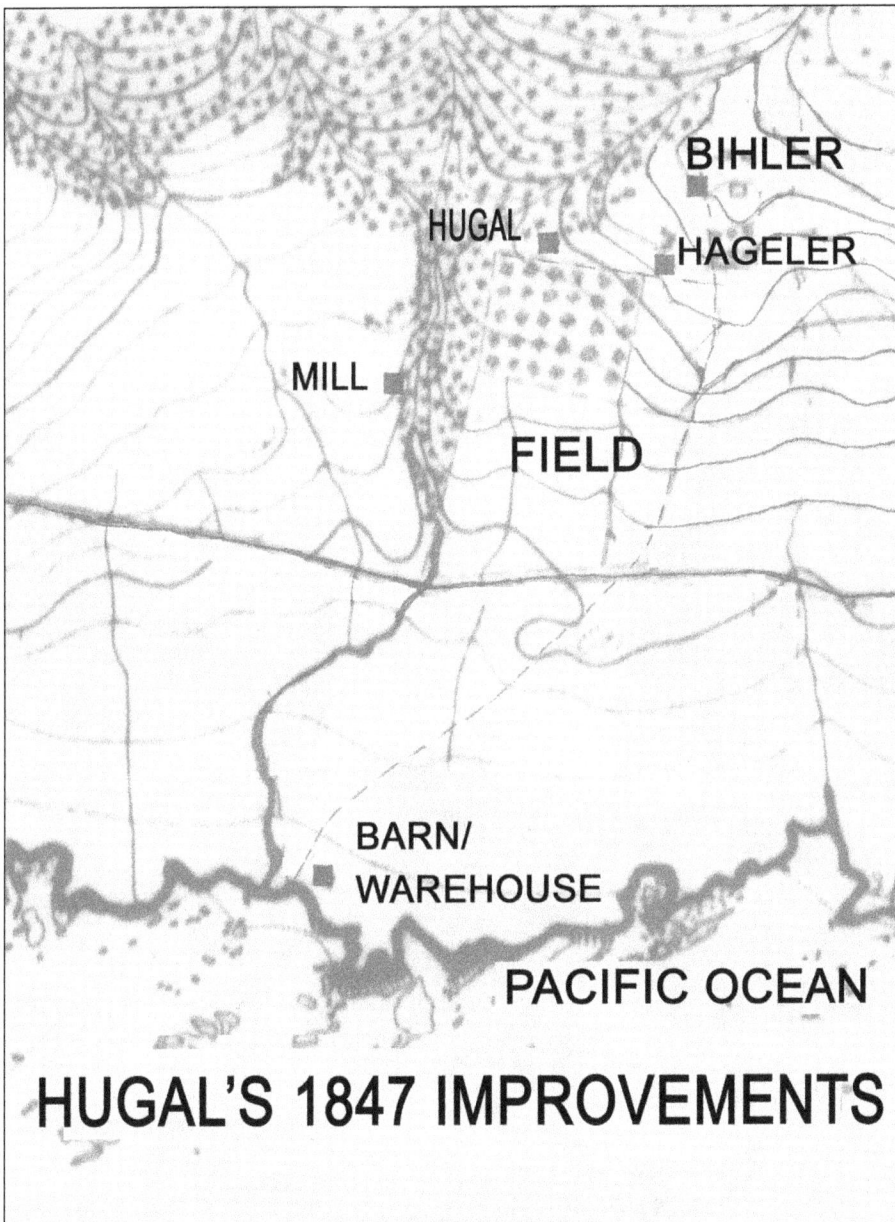

BIHLER

HUGAL

HAGELER

MILL

FIELD

BARN/
WAREHOUSE

PACIFIC OCEAN

HUGAL'S 1847 IMPROVEMENTS

Ernest Rufus promised Frederick Hugal and Henry Hageler that both of them would receive 1 1/4 leagues of his German Rancho grant. He would retain 1 1/4 league for himself. The men assumed that the grant measured approximately 5 leagues long and 1 league deep. When Rufus discovered that Hugal had settled on prime, unforested land, he decided to reduce Hugal's share to 1 league. Hugal built a cabin on a knoll alongside a creek above today's Knipp Stengel Barn. By 1847, William Bihler and Henry Hageler built cabins nearby. The first surveyed map of the rancho lands was not produced until 1861 when the United States sent out a professional surveyor. The survey revealed a conflict between what the original grantees understood and what later deeds described regarding parcel boundaries. By that time, there had been several transfers of ownership. When disagreements led to lawsuits in the 1870s, this map showing improvements on Hugal's land by 1847 was submitted as an exhibit.

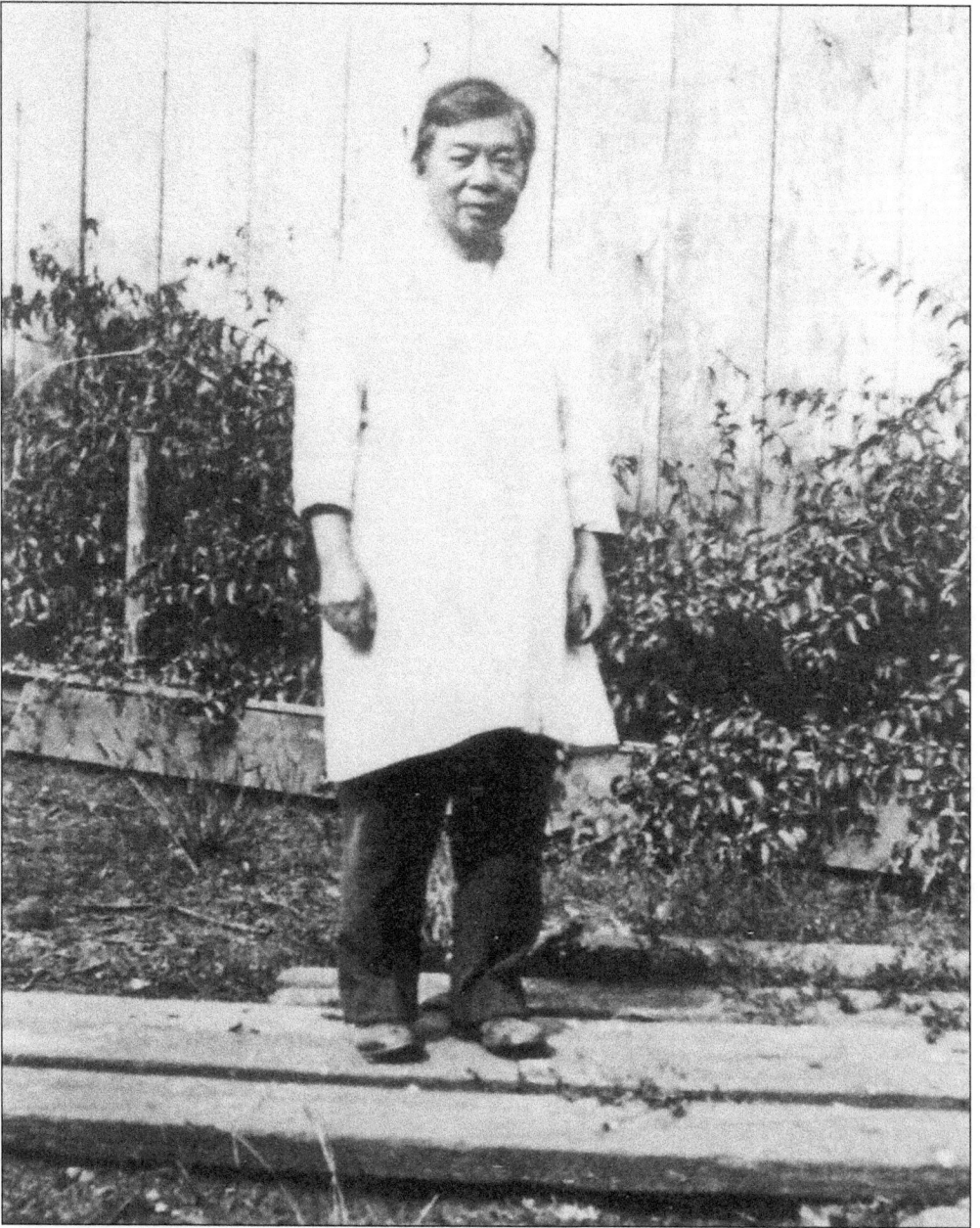

In the 1870s and 1880s, there were often more Chinese immigrants living on the German Rancho than there were Anglos. Many of the young, single Chinese men came to the United States during the Gold Rush and later turned to working on the transcontinental railroad. Following the completion of the railroad in 1869, many made their way to the northern Sonoma coast and took on the difficult work of logging for the lumber companies. Most of them lived together in boardinghouses or in logging camps. Almost every household on the northern coast employed at least one Chinese worker to cook or keep house. The Chinese servant sometimes took charge of rearing a man's children after the death of his wife. The domestically employed Chinese were often considered an important part of the home and were often included in family snapshots. This photograph, taken about 1910, shows Ah Ching, who worked for the Richardson family.

When Chris Stengel and Adam Knipp assumed management of Bihler's property on the German Rancho in 1859, they moved into the small house Bihler had built on the knoll near Hugal. Stengel and Knipp had made enough money to have a more comfortable home by the 1870s. Their new one-and-a-half story home was framed with redwood and sided with boards and battens, which were painted white. The home was built around a central staircase and featured a brick fireplace, which provided heat for the north-end rooms. There were two narrow, gable roof dormers, which looked out over the front entry. The full-width open porch was supported by six paired posts. The centered entry door was flanked by tall, double-hung wooden windows. The interior of the home was welcoming, with thick-looped wool Brussels carpet in the parlor. Paintings decorated the walls. The men's rooms opened from the parlor. Their bedroom furniture was made from black walnut and the bedding from fine, white linen. Beginning in the 1860s, Stengel employed a Chinese cook but never a housekeeper or servant. He and Knipp performed the household chores.

By the time they were ready to retire, at the end of the 19th century, Chris Stengel and Adam Knipp had developed an extensive livestock ranch. Their major ranch buildings were located at the foot of the knoll where they made their home. Sonoma County had made improvements to the still unpaved coast road in the 1870s. In the 1890s, the Gualala River was bridged, which enabled Stengel to transport dairy products north without being at the mercy of Niles Rufus, the cranky ferryman who operated the ferry near the mouth of the Gualala River. A large dairy barn was built close to the coast road to facilitate the loading and unloading of milk cans. The photograph above shows fences, which ran along both sides of the coast road and passed between cultivated fields and the fenced corals where the dairy cows grazed. The photograph below is a close-up view of the cluster of buildings with the Knipp Stengel Barn at the far right and the hay barn, which are still preserved on The Sea Ranch.

Robert Rutherford farmed the northern 985 acres near the mouth of the Gualala River in the 1870s and 1880s. He built a dairy barn, seen above, in the 1880s when he expanded operations to include a dairy. He began leasing a portion of his land in 1873 to Joe Tongue, a Finnish fruit grower who lived in Gualala. Unfortunately, when Rutherford took out a mortgage for the last parcel in 1882, he used the entire 985 acres as collateral. By 1894, he was behind in his payments and tried to raise money by selling off part of his land to Redwood Lumber Company. Nevertheless, the bank foreclosed on the loan in 1894. After foreclosure, the property was held by Cornelius Shea of the Santa Rosa Savings Bank, who renewed Tongue's lease in 1895. Tongue planted the Rutherford's fields with vegetables and grains. Sometime around 1890, Tongue constructed a landing on the rocky ocean bluff directly behind Rutherford's barn. The photograph below shows Tongue's landing with bags of grain ready to be shipped.

Barns were built wherever they were needed for ranching during the 19th century. The small horse barn shown in this photograph was constructed of redwood on the lower western edge of the knoll where the Knipp Stengel Barn now sits. It was the oldest of the buildings shown in the lower photograph on page 16 of this book. It measured approximately 40 feet by 50 feet and rested on cut log sections. It was mainly built of reused hand-hewn timbers with mortice and tenon joinery. The barn had vertical board siding and a gable roof covered with split-wood shakes. It backed up to the most western of the cypress trees in the short hedgerow but was considerably older than the trees. It was used as a machine shop during the 20th century. By 1986, it had severely deteriorated and was demolished by The Sea Ranch Association in preparation for the development of the lots in Unit 36.

Two

LOGGING THE REDWOODS
1880–1910

Brothers William and George Bender's construction of a mill and landing at Del Mar in 1898 ushered in a decade of activity at the north end of the Knipp Stengel Ranch. The mill foreman, Hans Petersen, moved into the house previously occupied by Robert Rutherford and his family. The mill and accessory buildings were constructed on the point to the northwest of the foreman's house. The settlement included many aspects of a small town. A company store was built on the coast road inland from the mill. Nearby was a warehouse and across the road was the saloon. Fences ran along both sides of the coast road, and a gate in the fence opened to a narrow, unpaved road that led down to the mill. Small mill workers' cabins dotted the meadow. A railroad line that paralleled the coast road terminated at the mill.

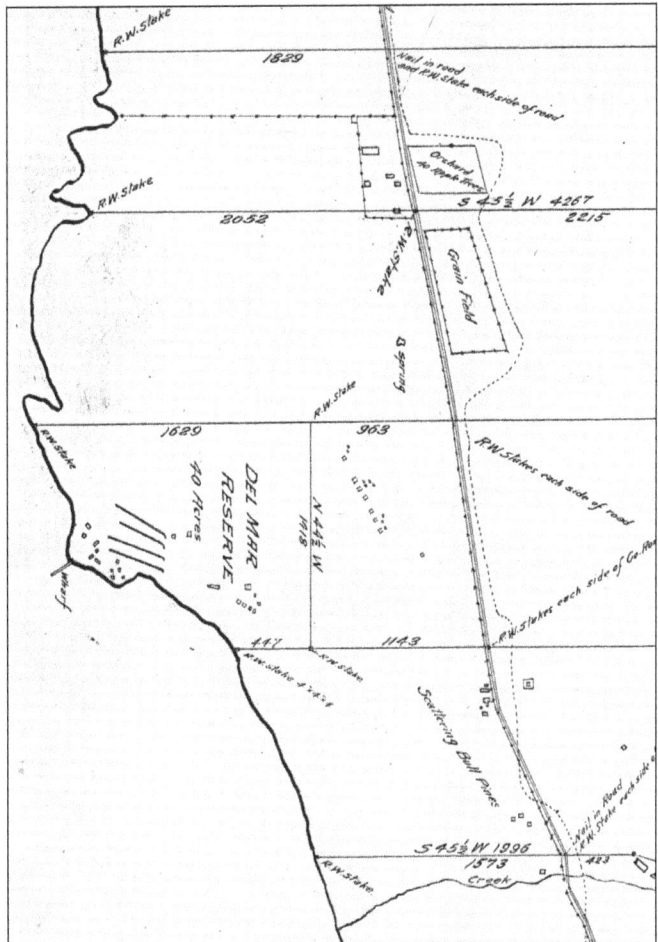

The above photograph was taken between 1905 and 1909, when bull teams pulled the newly cut logs to a log skid where they could be loaded on the upper terminus of the rail line. The log skid consisted of several parallel logs, which lay 8 to 12 inches apart on the ground. Once the logs arrived at the log skid, each log would be unhooked from the bull team and rolled across the log skid to be loaded onto a railcar, which would deliver it to the mill. When the train loaded with logs arrived at the Del Mar Mill, as shown in the photograph below, each log would be pushed off onto another log skid to facilitate moving it from the train to the mill. These skids at Del Mar were still in place until the 1980s when the construction crews who were installing new streets and sewer lines in Unit 34C parked heavy equipment on them one evening and smashed the worn, softened redwood logs.

There were many more employees working at the Del Mar Mill than those who lived in the immediate area. Some men came from Annapolis and others from Gualala. The mill company constructed and operated a cookhouse for the men at Del Mar next to the mill. Logging crews stopped work when the lunch whistle blew. The men were gathered in front of the cookhouse when this photograph was taken sometime between 1905 and 1910.

Wooden trestles like this were elevated above ground in several places along the rail line, which delivered logs to the Del Mar Mill. Tracks ran across the meadows from the mill to the ravine just north of the Knipp Stengel Barn. From there, temporary short spur tracks ran up ravines and delivered timber on flat railcars back down to the rail line. After all the accessible timber was taken from an area, the spur tracks were taken up and relocated to another area.

The machine shop at Del Mar was deteriorated when the photograph above was taken in 1941. Between 1900 and 1910, equipment for the Del Mar Mill was fabricated and repaired at the machine shop, which stood near the bluff to the south of the mill. Fortunately when the mill burned in 1910, the machine shop was just far enough away that it was not damaged by the fire. The steam power plant for the mill is seen in the photograph below. After the mill burned, the power plant was pushed off the bluff onto the beach below the machine shop. Occasionally at times of very low tides, the power plant can be seen on the sand.

Built of redwood in about 1899, the Del Mar Store sat on the west side of the coast road. Although 50 years would pass before electric wires came to the coast, telephone service was offered at the store by the Sunset Telephone Company. Mill workers and other locals used charge accounts to buy dry goods and get cash advances. The clerk and purchasing agent, Orin Gillmore, entered every transaction in a ledger. The ledger records a $22 purchase by Knipp and Stengel for a ton of barley on November 23, 1899. The same month Knipp and Stengel sold 367 pounds of beef to the store for $25.69. Entries in the store ledger tell something about other facilities associated with the mill and landing, such as the mill cookhouse, woods cookhouse, saloon, stable, and blacksmith shop. The photograph was taken in 1909 when Frank Glynn and Hans Petersen were operating the Del Mar Mill. Frank Glynn is seen in front of the door wearing suit and hat.

In 1898, Bender Mill and Lumber Company established a lumber mill on the bluff near Del Mar Point. Within a couple of years, the mill was in full operation and employed dozens of woodsmen to bring the lumber down from the hills and many mill workers. The tall stacks seen in both photographs are a reminder that all power to operate the mill machinery was generated by steam. The mill workers gathered in front of the mill to have the picture above taken about 1909. Some of the men in the above photograph have been identified. Frank Glynn, a mill supervisor, is shown in a suit and with a pipe. To his right are Bill Curtis, Lon Hoods, unidentified, and Sid Baker. In the top row, the man fifth from left is Lou Petersen (nephew of an owner) and ninth from left in a striped shirt is Burr Glynn (son of Frank). The photograph below shows how close the mill sat to the rocky bluff edge.

When the time came for the noon break, the woods crew gathered at the cookhouse in the above photograph. The outdoor cookhouse was nothing more than an open, sloped-top framework that was covered during the rainy season so the woodsmen would not have to eat in the rain. The Chinese cook was the star of the show. He planned the meals and transported the food in large baskets up the hill into the woods. He cooked over a nearby open fire and served from a small table between the fire and the long wooden tables. The 35 or so men crowded together on narrow benches on each side of two long wood-plank tables. When the men were done, the cook washed the dishes. The photograph below was taken April 9, 1911, in the Del Mar woods. Emil Hast is sitting near the steam donkey holding the lantern.

SUBSCRIPTION RATES:
One year, in advance, - - - $2.00
Six months, in advance, - - 1.00
Three months, in advance, - - .50

Entered as second class mail matter at the postoffice at Mendocino, California under the Act of Congress of March 2, 1908.

SATURDAY July 9, 1910.

A SAD ENDING

DEL MAR MILL WAS INSURED FOR $15,000

Blaze Supposed to Have Started From a
Spark From Locomotive. Other
Items From the Record.
Was Operated On

Ernest Farrer, 20 years old son of a Boonville merchant, had an attack of appendicitis last week, it was the fourth attack within a few months. Dr. Huntly watched the case carefully for twelve hours and concluded an operation would be necessary so started about 9 o'clock Tuesday evening with Ernest for San Francisco They arrived in Cloverdale about 12 o'clock and took the first train to the city, reaching the hospital at 12m. and the operation was performed at once disclosing a sloughing appendix. The doctor came back to Boonville the same day, making the round trip in just a little over 24 hours, and brought the diseased organ home with him. The patient is having an uneventful recovery

The Del Mar mill was destroyed by fire Monday. It is believed that sparks from the locomotive used in hauling ties to the landing started the fire, several blazes having been discovered and extinguished recently

The mill had not been operated for some time, and probably never would have been again, but Glenn & Peterson are losers on the machinery and other materials. The loss is said to be about $40,000 with an insurance of $15,000

The baseball game on the local diamond the first of the week between Greenwood and Point Arena teams resulted in a victory for the latter by a score of 16 to 3

Twelve years after it was constructed on the bluff at Del Mar, the Del Mar Mill burned. Frank Glynn and Hans Petersen had been operating the mill since Bender Mill and Lumber Company went into receivership in 1904. All the timber that was easily accessible had already been cut for the more than 40 years that logging had been carried out in the Del Mar woods. The woodsmen were working over the stumps of previously fallen trees to produce wood shakes, shingles, and railroad ties. No big timber remained. The Gualala Mill Company had already sold out to a group of Arkansas and Louisiana lumbermen in 1903. They operated the mill as the Empire Redwood Company until it burned in September 1906. The big logging days on this section of the coast ended until a new mill opened in the 1940s.

Three

STEAMERS, STAGES, AND RAILS
1870–1920

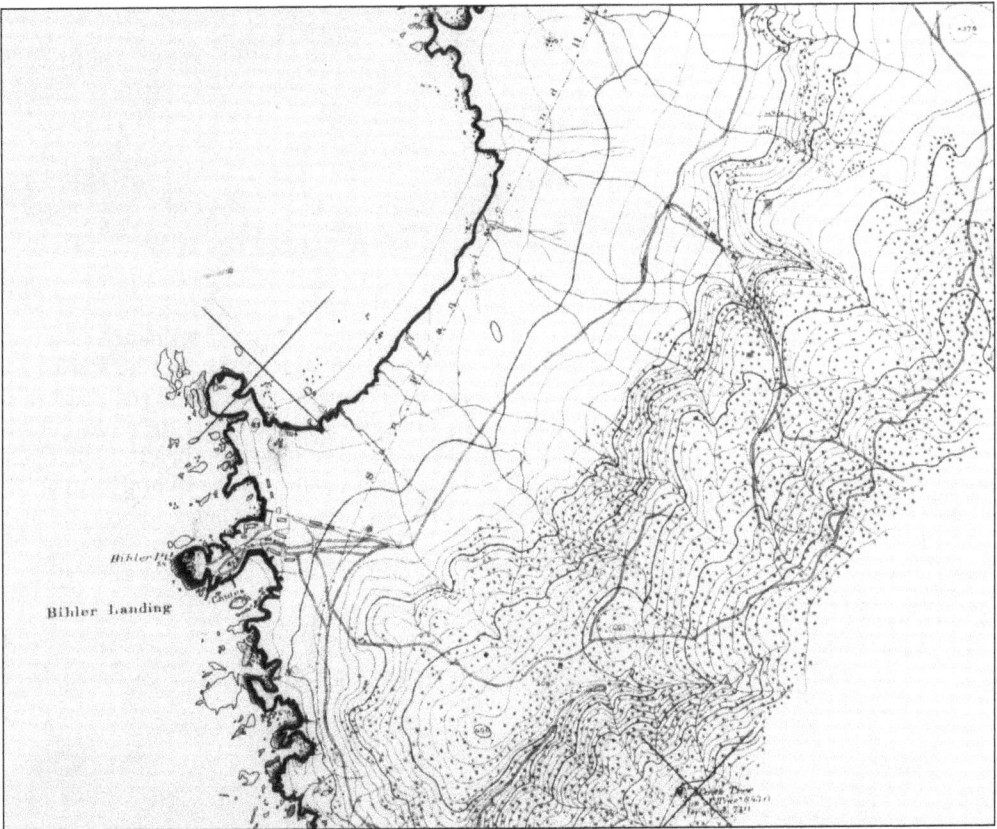

The Black Point area experienced rapid growth when two chutes were constructed on the south side of Bihler Point in the late 1870s. When the U.S. Coast and Geodetic Survey surveyed this area of the coast in late 1878 and early 1879, there were at least a dozen buildings near the landing, including a hotel, livery, blacksmith shop, sheds, and other miscellaneous structures. The landing was heavily used to ship produce and small wood products from Annapolis. The San Francisco telegraph line can be seen just inland from the coast. Several short roads led from the coast road west toward Black Point. Two roads branch off to the east from the coast road. The southernmost one leads up the hill and eventually connects with Annapolis Road. The northernmost road passes by a logging camp before continuing into the timberlands. The land terraces and edge of the timberline are also evident in this map produced by the U.S. Coast and Geodetic Survey.

Above is a *c.* 1880 sketch by artist and lumberman Charles Nystrom, which shows the chutes and landing at Black Point. The photograph below, dating from the 1890s, shows a schooner tied-up at Bihler Landing. George Davidson with the U.S. Coast and Geodetic Survey described the landing in the 1889 *Coast Pilot*. He wrote that the "vessel lies broadside to the end [of the chute] with six mooring-lines. There are breakers close under the starboard bow of the vessel at the chute and breakers to the eastward only fifty yards distant. The swell affects the vessel at the chute. There are three mooring buoys. The inner one of them is one hundred yards southeast of the outer chute, and lies in five or six fathom of water, with a rock above water thirty yards northeast and a sunken rock with eleven feet upon it seventy yards southeast. This is a summer landing only, and an average of five small schooners per month load wood, posts, tan-bark, and stave-bolts. Three vessels may lie at anchor in the cove, but the place is dangerous from October to June."

During the 1880s and 1890s, Knipp and Stengel managed the landing facilities at Bihler's Landing. There was a hotel, saloon, blacksmith shop, store, post office, livery, and warehouse for the landing wire. The warehouse had a tongue-and-groove pine floor for dancing. Martin Cook was a local fiddler who played for the dances. The morning after a dance, the dance floor was swept out, covered with 2-inch planking, and the warehouse was returned to housing the wire. The post office, known as "Fisherman's Bay," was located at Stewarts Point from 1863 until 1889 when it was moved to Black Point. During the 1890s, when Knipp and Stengel expanded their operations, they incorporated as the Fisherman's Bay Commercial Company. In the photograph above, dating from the 1890s, locals and visitors are seen gathering in front of the store, hotel, and post office, which were operated by the Fisherman's Bay Commercial Company. The blacksmith shop at Black Point is below.

During the 19th century, when transporting products by schooner was dependent upon the weather and there was no paved coast road, enterprising individuals and lumber companies endeavored to lay railroad tracks and build railroad trestles along the coast to cross rivers, ravines, and gulches. There were ferries, which crossed the Russian River and the mouth of the Gualala River, but they were unable to carry heavy loads of lumber and large wagonloads of tanbark, fruit, and vegetables. After easily accessible timber near the coast was harvested, lumber mills sought forested areas farther inland. The short line from Clipper Mill delivered lumber products to Stewarts Point landing for transport. A railroad trestle was constructed across the South Fork of the Gualala River near present-day Hauser Bridge.

Situated at the far northwest corner of the county and at a distance from cities and commercial activities of Sonoma County, the coast road was pretty much ignored by Sonoma County officials. The stage route for passengers and mail ran between Mendocino and Cazadero, where the stage was met by the Northwestern Pacific Railroad, which connected with points inland. Starting at Mendocino, the stage would drive as far as Elk and then change horses. Horses were changed again at Point Arena and Gualala. It would continue onto Stewarts Point where horses would be changed again before traveling down the coast road to the turn off for Plantation; after stopping at Plantation, the stage driver would turn south on Sea View Road, where he stopped again for fresh horses and then took the road down to Cazadero. The photograph above shows Raymond and his horse Jack driving the mail stage. The photograph below was taken of the passenger stage, which brought visitors from Cazadero. A ride to San Francisco took two days.

Northern Sonoma coast residents not only endured poor roads to get to Santa Rosa and inland towns, they were also limited in going north for lack of a bridge across the Gualala River. Mendocino County officials proposed bridging the river as early as the 1870s. On March 27, 1878, the governor of California signed legislation providing $3,000 for construction of a bridge across the Gualala River, but Sonoma County officials were not interested. Sonoma County officials cared more about easing transportation to and from the Bay Area rather than paying for a bridge located where few county residents ever traveled. As a result, the Gualala River was not bridged until 1892, when a lightweight wagon bridge was constructed just east of the present bridge. In 1906, photographer François Matthes took the image above, which documented a substantial drop of the end of the bridge, which occurred when the 1906 earthquake caused the south approach to collapse. The photograph below was taken in 1919 when a new bridge over the Gualala River was under construction.

Until the coast road was paved and designated as a state highway, a bridge spanned McClellan Gulch, the first ravine south of Stewarts Point. The gulch and bridge were named for Michael McClellan who came to the area with his wife in 1860 and built a house just south of Stewarts Point. That same year, a notorious murder took place near McClellan's place. Several members of the Stewart family were implicated in the shooting of Davenport Helms. Testimony from the trial was presented verbatim in the *Sonoma County Democrat*. The U. S. Surveyor General had not yet opened for sale the public land of Salt Point Township. Conflicts over ownership and land titles were already resulting in violence.

This photograph of the coast road was taken after 1903, when the first telephone lines went in, and before the early 1920s, when the road was paved. The work was very labor intensive with short scrapers pulled by a pair of horses. The roadway was first scraped and then rolled, or compacted. There was no top coat or sealing material, so as soon as the first rain arrived, the road would become a muddy quagmire. Without a top coat of asphalt, wagons, stages, and teams of horses would leave deep ruts in the road. Traveling down the coast was an uncomfortable dirty experience.

Residents along the coast were more passionate about improving transportation inland. The port that accommodated most of the commercial business was at Point Arena, and the road between northern Sonoma County and Point Arena was windy, difficult, and required negotiating gullies and ravines. Bull teams and later short line rails were used by lumber companies to haul timber to the mill. Sonoma County made small improvements to the coast road beginning in the 1870s. The narrow, windy, unpaved roads and bridges presented problems when automobiles and heavy-duty trucks became more prevalent. When plans to pave the road from Jenner to the Mendocino County line were announced, coastal residents gladly offered easements over their property and contributed to the cost of the road. Arch and Font, sons of Herbert A. Richardson, were hired by the county to construct the road. The photograph on this page was taken of Arch Richardson and the Holt 25 tractor at the end of McClellan Bridge in 1921. The tractor was too heavy to traverse the bridge across the gulch. Arch Richardson was the road boss. The woman is Anna Richardson. The crawler was new and belonged to Sonoma County.

The accessible timbered areas had been extensively logged from about 1860 through the early days of the 20th century. Woodsmen frequently stayed in the area when the large logs were gone and worked the stumps and the smaller trees that were left behind. They would often remain as employees of the lumber company and would produce fence posts, tanbark, railroad ties, and shakes. These products were called, "small stuff." The small stuff was loaded onto wagons drawn by two horses. Upon arriving at Black Point, the horses would be rewarded with the food bag before beginning their trip back to the Del Mar woods. The long bark teams waiting to unload are seen above. In the photograph below, the driver waits while the horses get their rewards.

The coast road just north of the Knipp Stengel Barn was cut into a loose clay embankment. Before the road was paved, the road in this area would be impassable when the first rains came. Locals referred to this section as the clay pitches. The above photograph was taken in the early 1920s. Besides soil challenges, Sonoma County also had to confront the problem posed by the steep fall off if there was to be a road constructed along the coast. Finally, Richardson Brothers, who owned several pieces of big machinery, entered into a contact with the county to construct the road. Upon its completion about 1926, when County Route 56 was taken over by the state, it was renamed State Highway One. The photograph below was taken shortly after the road was completed.

At the beginning of the 20th century, when the lumber industry faded, residents moved away from the village that had grown at Black Point. In 1902, the last ship sailed out of Bihler Landing and the Fisherman's Bay Post Office closed. Black Point hotel had very few guests, and the building suffered neglect and deterioration. Workers looked for new jobs in Gualala, Annapolis, and Stewarts Point. When the county sent surveyors to survey the roadway in 1922, a note describing Black Point was entered in the transit book. The notation reads, "A clutter of tumbledown houses and fences that used to be Black Point Landing." The photographs on this page show the condition of the hotel and other buildings in 1920.

A dramatic change came to the coast in 1915 when Jack Caylor arrived behind the wheel of the first motor-driven stage. The tall man in the photograph was longtime coast resident Henry Case. Like the horse-drawn stage before it, the motor-driven stage ran between Cazadero and Mendocino, making stops at Sea View, Plantation, Stewarts Point, Gualala, Point Arena, and Elk.

The *Klamath* went on the rocks just south of Del Mar Landing early in 1921. The crew hooked a cable between the ship and the shore and unloaded about 21 passengers. Marion Philbrik and his wife were living in a small house at Del Mar. Mrs. Philbrik was shocked that a lady came ashore without wearing stockings. She offered the woman her own stockings, but the woman declined and told her she had come ashore stocking-less and would leave the same way.

Stmr. klamath Wrecked Near
Stewarts Point, Calif.

An unexpected storm brought 75-knot winds and gusting rain to the Northern California coast in February 1921. The steamer *Klamath* was on her way to Portland when she was caught in the storm and crashed on the rocks just south of Del Mar Landing. She was carrying 19 passengers, including 1 baby, and 34 officers and crew. The captain ordered full speed astern, but the *Klamath* backed into other rocks, which caused even more damage. An SOS call went out, and *Klamath*'s sister ships *Everett* and *Curacao* responded, but they were unable to pull *Klamath* back out to sea. A cable with a breeches buoy was arranged to get people ashore. At first, the baby presented a problem. Then a member of the crew wrapped the baby in blankets, put the wrapped baby in a garbage can, and put the can in the breeches buoy for the trip to safety.

Klamath did not immediately sink and disappear from sight. As the weeks passed, travelers along the coast road continued to watch for activity on the ship. By the time it was apparent that the *Klamath* could not be returned to sea, the salvage ship *Cadet* arrived with a crew of eight men for salvaging. When the job was done, the salvage crew paused before returning home and held up the *Klamath* nameplate for a photograph (below). Finally after a couple of months, the ship broke up and sank.

From 1892 to 1906, the wooden
bridge that crossed the Gualala River
allowed residents of northern Sonoma
and southern Mendocino counties
to go back and forth if they could
manage the unpaved roads, which
made the trip uncomfortable. The
bridge, seen in the above photograph,
sat to the east of the present bridge,
almost to Switchville. After 1910,
automobiles were seen occasionally
passing through the coastal towns.
It soon became apparent that the
wooden bridge was not strong enough
to bear the weight of cars or heavily
loaded vehicles. The photograph at
left was taken in 1919, when a new
bridge was being constructed.

Four

STEWARTS POINT AND THE RICHARDSON FAMILY
1870–2009

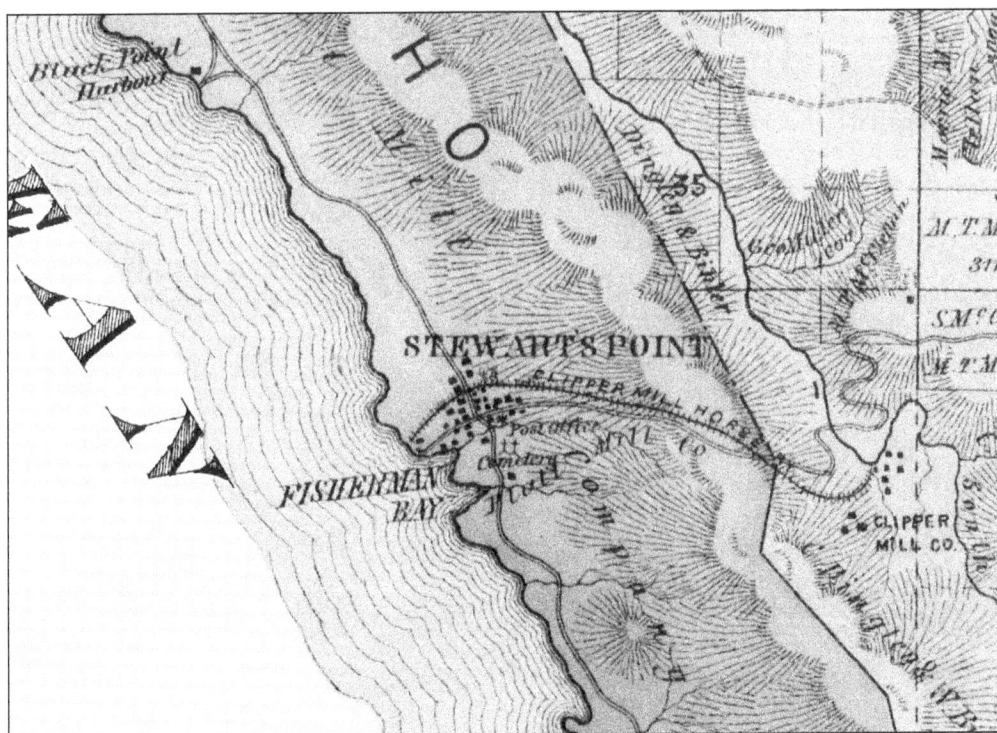

The development of Stewarts Point is seen on a map from the 1877 *Historical Illustrated Atlas of Sonoma County*. More than 30 buildings were located near the intersection of Skaggs Springs Road and coast highway. The Fisherman's Bay Post Office was located at Stewarts Point at that time, not having yet been relocated to Black Point. The Clipper Mill horse-drawn railroad brought milled lumber from the woods down to the landing at Stewarts Point. The Clipper Mill operated near the south bank of the Gualala River. Stewarts Point Store was already in business, and a cemetery was established.

The photograph above is one of the earliest taken of Stewarts Point. The hotel had not yet been constructed. The Richardson residence is at the left and the store on the right. John C. Fisk owned Stewarts Point in the 1860s and 1870s, when the photograph was taken. Fisk wrote letters to Herbert A. (H. A.) Richardson, who lived in New Hampshire, urging him to come to the Sonoma coast. Richardson and his bride, Althea, arrived in California in 1878, and H. A. began working as a bartender for Fisk at Stewarts Point. Within a couple of years, H. A. bought out Fisk and took over operating the dry goods store. Richardson purchased thousands of acres of timberland from Stewarts Point to the Mendocino County line. He built a lumber mill, a railroad, and a landing, which is seen below. He owned several schooners, which transported lumber from the mill to ports along the coast.

Stewarts Point Landing was an important port of call from the late 19th century to 1923, when it ceased operation. H. A. Richardson controlled much of the north coast lumber market for many years and built both shipping facilities and a horse-drawn rail line to facilitate the transportation of lumber products. One of the schooners who stopped regularly at Stewarts Point was the *Portia*. The photograph above was taken when the *Portia* went ashore there in 1899 before she was again pulled out to sea. The photograph below shows the steamer *Vanguard* in Stewarts Point cove. The *Vanguard* was one of many steamers owned by H. A. Richardson beginning in 1880. Richardson had steamers named for his daughter, the *Gracie Belle Richardson*, and sons, the *Archie* and *Fontie*. Stewarts Point was a frequent stop for the following schooners: *Abe Lincoln, Bender Brothers, Bessie K., Black Prince, Charles T. Winslow, Corinthian, Daisy Rowe, Emma and Louise, Lottie Collins, Mary Etta, Reliance, Rio Rey,* and *Rosie Sparks*.

At the turn of the 20th century, the Richardson's Stewarts Point was the local Wells Fargo stop. Sunset Telephone Company ran a line on the coast in 1902 and Stewarts Point had one of the very few telephones where people could pay to make a call. Herbert A. Richardson's General Merchandise offered basic supplies to locals. A few items from the store ledger dated from November 1899 to January 31, 1900, are as follows: 15 pounds of sugar: $1; 4 rolls butter: $1.80; 9.5 pounds of beef: 95¢; 1 pair shoes: $3; 1 box of cartridges: 15¢; and 1 pair of overalls: 75¢. The photograph on this page shows a man arriving with a wagon and team of six horses. The bells on the horses announced the team and rider as they approached blind curves ahead.

Since Herbert A. Richardson and his wife, Althea, bought Stewarts Point in 1878, their descendants have lived and worked there. In the above photograph, taken in the 1890s, a two-story gable addition had been constructed on the west side of the original farmhouse. A wooden porch wrapped around the second story and provided a roof for the lower open porch. The hotel guests posing on the porch all appear to be men. Vines and climbing roses are growing up the east elevation of the hotel. In the photograph below two women are standing on the porch of the residence adjacent to the hotel. The logs seen at the end of the porch in front of the two women served as a step for those who arrived in horse-drawn stages or in wagons.

After they arrived at Stewarts Point, H. A. Richardson and Althea had three children: Gracie Belle, born 1879; Archie, born 1886; and Fontaine, born 1889. Eventually, Gracie married and moved to Healdsburg. Archie and Fontaine remained on the coast, married, and had children. The photograph at left, taken in 1915, shows Archie (Archer Herbert) Richardson and his wife, Anna, with their first child, Don, who was born in 1914. The photograph below shows Don and his sister, Julia, born four years later, and Archer (known all his life as Bus), who came two years after Julia. Bus operated the Stewarts Point store and the post office for over 40 years. He was a friend to the long-term coastal residents, the Kashaya, and The Sea Ranch newcomers. If there was one name associated with the coast in the second half of the 20th century, it was Bus Richardson.

In 1920, when H. A. Richardson's older son Archie was managing the Stewarts Point store, the above photograph was taken of his children: two-year-old Julia and six-year-old Don Richardson enjoying their ride on Paso. In the photograph below, dated 1922, Don Richardson and Marian Ball Miller are seen in a horse cart in front of Stewarts Point hotel. Marian was Donald's teacher at Stewarts Point School and also his cousin. Julia later married Don Richardson (no relation) and lived in a house near the coast road until her death in 1994.

During the 19th century, many women who lived in northern Sonoma County lived without the daily friendship of other women. They worked hard with their husbands on farms and single-handedly ran families with many children when their husbands were spending weeknights in lumber camps. It was not uncommon for a woman to die of infection shortly after the birth of a baby. When they did get a chance to get together, women offered each other comfort and shared laughs. In the photograph above, Priscilla Cole, who operated a saloon near Valley Crossing for many years, shares some fun with Anna Richardson. In the photograph below, seven women wait near Stewarts Point for the arrival of the motor-driven stage, which will take them down to Cazadero where it will connect with the North Pacific Railroad. From left to right are Marion Ball, Ina Ball, Cada Call, Emma Call, two unidentified, and Leah Eckert.

The Stewarts Point steam locomotive brought cut timber from along the South Fork of the Gualala River to Stewarts Point for loading on ships. The steam locomotive replaced the earlier horse-drawn railroad. After most of the big timber had been harvested in the 19th century, the woodsmen returned to the woods to rework the smaller trees and stumps of trees previously cut. The second harvest extended the lumber days into the second decade of the 20th century. It then died off until regrowth and new technology permitted it to resume again about 1940. The photographs on this page show the last steam locomotive being hauled out of the area in the early 1930s. The engine was loaded onto a 1931 one-and-a-half-ton Indiana truck for transport.

The railroad tracks required regular maintenance in an area where they were frequently covered by the slippage of loose earth. In the photograph at left, workmen are clearing the tracks for the Heisler locomotive. Eventually, the Heisler was sold to the Prather Mill in Lake County.

This view of the settlement at Stewarts Point is rarely seen. It was taken near the landing looking northeast. The west elevation of the two-story Stewart's Point Hotel is seen in the center of the photograph. The store is situated to the east of the hotel and is not seen in this image. The tallest structure in the center of the photograph is the water tank, which is still, in 2009, located at the north end of the store.

At the beginning of the 20th century, the buildings at Stewarts Point, which all faced south, appeared freshly painted. The road that ran from the coast road in the front of the buildings and then down to the landing was free from debris and potholes. The number of men suggests that all of the hotel rooms were occupied and that the Chinese hotel cook would have a full dining room that night. No doubt the men would visit the saloon, which faced the hotel, both before and after dinner. The railing has been removed from the second-story porch since this photograph was taken.

By the late 1920s, the coast road was paved, and it was possible for a family from the Bay Area to enjoy a weekend camping on the coast. The Richardsons provided a small campground, with a view of the ocean, which filled up with campers when the weather was not too cold. During the Depression days of the 1930s, camping was the only type of vacation affordable to many people. Automobiles and small tents are seen at the campground in this photograph.

This photograph dates from the early 1900s when members of the Kashaya Pomo were visiting Stewarts Point. Many Pomo families lived between the Russian and Gualala Rivers during the Russian occupation of Fort Ross during the first half of the 19th century and remained to work in the area after the Russians departed in 1841. By 1870, James Dixon, then owner of the Fort Ross property, forced the remaining Pomo off his land. With the Americans settling Salt Point Township and establishing farms, many Pomo had no place to go. Charles Haupt, an American who was married to a Kashaya woman, offered his wife's people a place to live on his property. By the beginning of the 20th century, Kashaya families lived at Haupt's ranch and near Stewarts Point, where they worked for the lumber companies. In 1914 at the request of the Kashaya, the Bureau of Indian Affairs purchased several acres about 5 miles east of Stewarts Point for a reservation. By 1919, most of the families were living on the reservation. Since moving north of Fort Ross in the 1870s, the Kashaya have relied on Stewarts Point for dry goods and postal services.

After the store at Stewarts Point passed from H. A. Richardson to his sons, the sign above the door was changed to read "Richardson Brothers General Merchandise." The store continued to buy products from and sell products to the local community. Beginning in the 1920s, the Richardsons had gas pumps installed to serve motorists on the coast. The photograph above shows 3.5-ton Indiana trucks hauling cordwood into Stewarts Point. In the 1930s, A. H. Richardson, H. A. Richardson's son, took over the store, and the sign was again repainted—this time to "A. H. Richardson General Merchandise." The picture below was taken in 1933 when a 1931 1.5-ton Studebaker truck pulled up to the front of the store with a load of poles, which would be used in the construction of a shed.

This photograph presents a comprehensive view of the settlement at Stewarts Point in 1926. The picture was taken from the southeast corner of the intersection of Skaggs Springs Road with Highway One. Skaggs Springs Road comes in from the right edge and Highway One runs through the middle of the photograph. At the far left is Stewarts Point Hotel. The equipment barn juts out behind it to the north. The Richardson Brothers' store is seen in the center. The water tank is seen to the north. Sitting behind the store and alongside the road is a small gable-roof building

with a single door. That is the Stewarts Point Post Office, which was later relocated across the highway. It still sits on a knoll across the highway, having been expanded with an addition in the 1980s. The gable-roof building that is seen on the east side of the highway is the harness shop. The white picket fence, which edges the highway and circles several buildings, presents a more manicured picture of Stewarts Point than is seen today.

The broad wooden steps, which stretch across the south-facing front of the Stewarts Point store, have always attracted locals as a place to sit and visit. Beginning in the 1870s and continuing to the present, Stewarts Point has been the gateway to the Knipp Stengel Ranch, the Del Mar Ranch, and now The Sea Ranch. For decades on Friday afternoons, when the workweek ended, local residents and those who had come up to Sea Ranch for the weekend, informally gathered and engaged in small talk. The photographs on this page, which date from the 1930s, indicate that the front porch and steps served the same function 70 years ago.

Five

FIRST FAMILIES AND FARMS
1904–1941

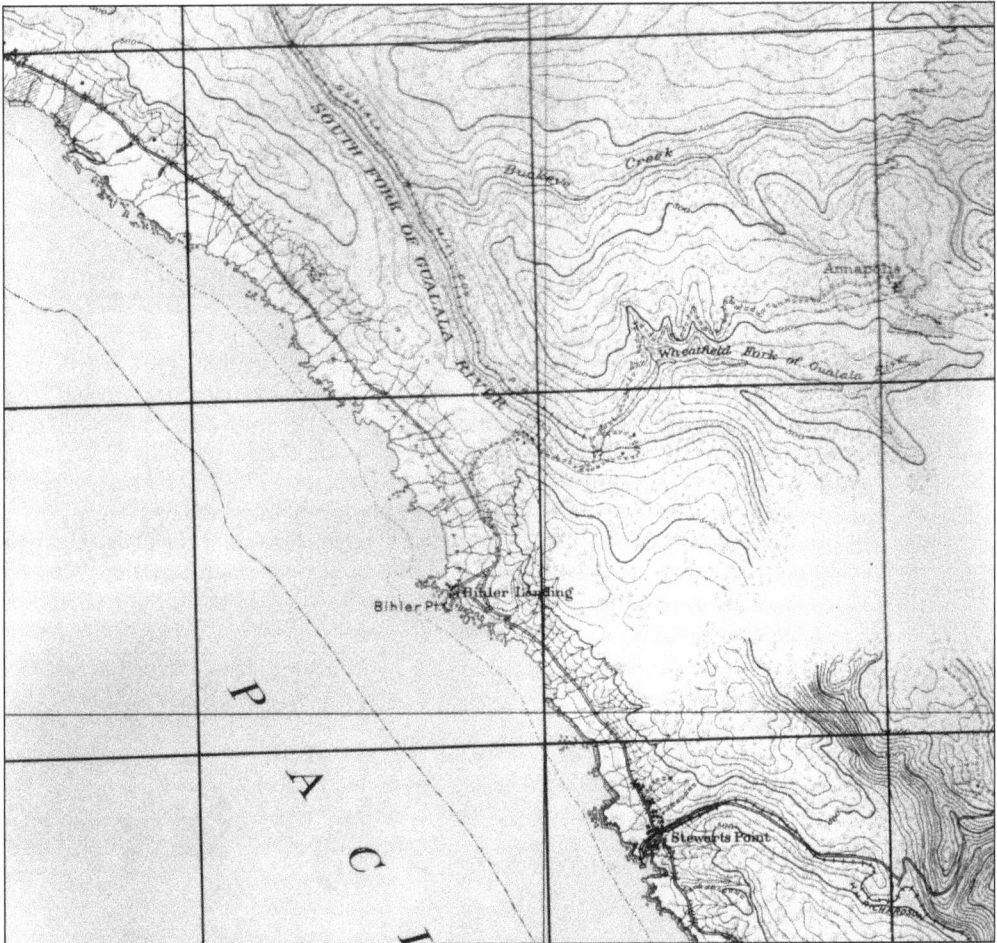

This map is a section of the 1921 fifteen-minute USGS topographic map "Plantation." The area was surveyed by the Army Corps of Engineers in 1915. It stops short of including the very north part of the ranch but gives information regarding the topography, roads, and development areas, such as Stewarts Point, Black Point, and the eucalyptus crown above the Knipp Stengel Barn. The Gualala Mill railroad is seen as it comes down from the north alongside the Gualala River until it terminates at Valley Crossing. Likewise, the route of Richardson's railroad from Stewarts Point is shown. At the far north end are a few of the buildings remaining from the settlement at Del Mar.

Between 1900 and 1910, three major activities came to an end. Shipping ceased from Bihler's Landing, milling ended at Del Mar, and Knipp and Stengel sold the ranch. In 1904, the Bender brothers, who purchased the entire Knipp Stengel Ranch, went bankrupt within a year, and trustees were appointed to sell off their assets. Howard Bishop and later Steven (Doug) Hamilton, both from Mendocino County, rented the house on the hill in the middle of the ranch that was formerly occupied by Christian Stengel and Adam Knipp. They raised livestock for a few years, knowing the property was for sale. They lived near the eucalyptus trees, which had already been planted on the hill, but their livestock roamed on windy, open meadows since the hedgerows had not yet been planted. The above photograph of the Stengel house was taken between 1906 and 1910, when the Hamiltons were living there. The photograph below shows the Knipp Stengel Barn and the coast road, which sat below the house.

Between 1910 and 1920, many families moved away from the northern Sonoma–southern Mendocino coast. The mill at Del Mar had burned as had the big Gualala mill. In this photograph, which dates from about 1920, the river and the little town of Gualala are seen. Gualala was a company town, and when the lumber industry died so did the town. There were fewer mill workers to shop at the Gualala store, which sat on the west side of the road with a few other mill-owned buildings. Eventually, the store was pushed toward the river where it collapsed at the foot of the bank. Today it still sits there rotting under a wood-shingle gable roof. Most of the buildings in the photograph on the flat at the river bend were left over from the days when the mill operated. All that remained of the massive, three-story-tall Gualala mill, which was destroyed in a 1906 fire, was the foundation, which appears as a group of aligned racks in the center of the photograph.

Little Russian Girl Startles the Buddhists
Advent on Sacred Isle Breaks Traditions

Miyajima in Japan Had Suffered Dearth of Vital Statistics for Centuries.

EMELIAN NOSHKIN AND FAMILY

Vera Noshkin enjoys a unique distinction which marks her as an epoch maker in the history of Japanese religious rites.

Vera is the twenty days' old daughter of Emelian and Mrs. Noshkin, a Russian merchant and his wife, who arrived here from the Orient yesterday on the liner Persia.

The Noshkin family left Amur, Siberia, some weeks ago for San Francisco, where the wealthy merchant hopes to start a flour factory. While en route from Kobi to Yokohama on the Japanese steamer Amaricusa, the ship stopped at Miyajima, the famous sacred island of the Inland sea.

Mr. and Mrs. Noshkin landed at the island, and while there the baby, Vera, was born.

As far as history relates, no one has been born and no one has died on this sacred island. For countless centuries the island has been regarded as enchanted by the Japanese. But little Vera has broken all rules of tradition by making her first appearance in the world amid the sunny groves of Miyajima.

Noshkin brings with him to San Francisco eleven children, the eldest of whom is a beautiful girl of twenty summers. The boys are healthy and strong.

The *San Francisco Examiner* reported in its April 25, 1912, issue about the unexpected birth of a baby while the Noshkin family was sailing from Russia to the United States. A group of Russian Baptists headed by Emelian Noshkin arrived in San Francisco in 1912. They were escaping the religious persecution and political chaos occurring in Russia. Noshkin's wife, Mary, delivered her 12th child during the journey. Within weeks of his arrival, Noshkin was informed that Bay Area businessman Walter Frick owned about 5,000 acres on the Sonoma coast that was available. Actually, Frick had just purchased the Del Mar Ranch from the Bender Lumber Company trustees when he heard the Russians were looking for property. By July 1912, Noshkin and about 500 Russians settled on the Del Mar Ranch and immediately began planting fruits and vegetables. The colonists were industrious and enjoyed an abundant harvest. They shared their crops and offered pastureland to their Gualala neighbors. When Noshkin contracted with Frick to purchase the property, he naively agreed to pay many times what the property was worth. There was no way Noshkin could make the payments, and Frick foreclosed on the mortgage in 1913. Sadly, with fields full of crops ready for harvesting, Noshkin and the colonists were forced to leave in September 1913.

The Noshkins posed for this photograph about 1916. Nadia Frangos, a descendant, provided this photograph and attempted to identify members of the family. From left to right are Vera, born 1912; Luba, born 1908; Michael, born 1893; Benjamin, born 1904; Mary Shulin Noshkin, born 1873; Katherine, born 1898; Mary, born 1891; Theodore, born 1892; Emelian, born 1863; Victor, born 1907; Alexander, born 1901; and Nadia, born 1905.

All summer in 1912, Emil Noshkin and his group of 250 Russian colonists planted a variety of crops on the open fields where livestock had grazed. They ordered two steam traction engines, which finally arrived at Point Arena on the *Sea Foam* in September. On September 7, Noshkin, an aide, and 38-year-old Nicholas Podsakoff were bringing the engines down the coast road, when they had to make a sharp turn and immediately straighten to navigate a narrow bridge across Schooner Gulch. The men got out to see if the engine was too heavy for the bridge. When the bridge started to collapse, Noshkin and the aide were able to get out of the way, but Podsakoff was trapped and killed. A few days later, a sad group of colonists stood on the windy headland and buried Podsakoff on the bluff a few hundred yards north of Del Mar. They marked his grave with a circle of white stones. This photograph probably dates from the 1930s.

In 1893, Walter P. Frick, an 18-year-old man from Indiana, arrived in El Dorado County to work in the mines. From mining, he expanded into buying parcels with standing timber and then reselling to lumber companies. He was financially shrewd and by 1906 had earned enough to relocate to Oakland and establish his office as a mining engineer in the Union Savings Bank Building. That same year, he also became a timber broker for the Wheeler Lumber Company out of Medford, Oregon. He bought tens of thousands of acres in Sonoma and Mendocino Counties on behalf of Wheeler. Frick impulsively bought whatever he thought might be a profitable investment. Having bought timberland in northern Sonoma County for Wheeler, Frick was familiar with the property the trustees of Bender Mill and Lumber Company were trying to sell. When word reached Frick that a recent immigrant from Russia was seeking farmland, he quickly purchased the 5,000 acres at a reduced price and then offered it to Emil Noshkin at a highly inflated price. Frick swindled Noshkin, who was naive about property values and American business practices. After Noshkin defaulted on the mortgage, the property ended up back in Frick's hands.

For a few years, from 1916 to 1921, foreman Michael Williams, and later Albert Ball, raised a small band of sheep on Frick's ranch. Most of their efforts were put toward Frick's beef cattle. Then in 1921, Frick was persuaded that sheep could bring him more profits than cattle. Since World War I, the wool market was better than the beef market. The University of California at Davis had established a wool laboratory and occasionally offered some of its sheep for outside sale. Frick was inspecting sheep at the wool laboratory when he met Fred Sagehorn, who was working there. Their shared interest in the same flock of sheep led to Frick's hiring Sagehorn to come to his Del Mar Ranch and take over as ranch foreman. Between 1921 and 1929, Sagehorn increased the number Frick's sheep to 3,000. This photograph dates from about 1921 when Frick first put sheep on his ranch.

Walter Frick owned the Del Mar Ranch when he married Helen Fay in 1916. They resided in the Bay Area where Frick had his office and conducted most of his real estate transactions. Helen Fay gave birth to three children in the next three years: Robert, born 1917; Walter, born 1918; and Helen Jane, born 1919. Frick was always involved with his various business dealings and was not home much with his family. The family continued to live in the Bay Area and used the Del Mar ranch as a summer home. As soon as school let out each year, they would drive up from San Francisco and leave the children with a Chinese cook and Mrs. Schwartz, their governess. The parents would then drive back to San Francisco. The Chinese cook took time to enjoy the children. He is seen at left allowing Helen Jane to help him paint behind the house at Del Mar. The photograph below suggests a far more disciplined relationship between the children and Mrs. Schwartz.

Anyone who has spent a week at The Sea Ranch is aware of the wildlife in the area: deer, rabbits, raccoons, bobcats, foxes, and even an occasional mountain lion. A hundred years ago, elk and bear were also frequently seen. Elk have not been seen for decades but not so for bear. Even now, every once in a while Sea Ranchers will report finding bear paw scratches in their yards or seeing bears outside their windows at night. When Bert Steele heard reports of a bear roaming around the north end of the Del Mar Ranch in 1934, he set a trap. This photograph shows Steele with a bear he caught in a trap on the Del Mar Ranch in 1934.

Walter Frick successfully took the property from the Russians, but exactly what did he get? Not a beautiful pastoral landscape by any means. The wind-blown Del Mar Ranch (above) was overgrazed and carelessly logged. Intermittent railroad tracks ran from the landing at Del Mar to the drainage north of the Knipp Stengel Barn. Miles of fencing had been torn up and used by the Russians as fuel to feed their steam engines. The buildings that remained were mostly old and deteriorated. Frick's first thought was how he could generate a profit. He set about making the land more attractive for marketing. Beginning in 1916, he had Charlie Fiscus from Annapolis plant cypress hedgerows, which served as windbreaks and divided the land into 24 ranchettes of about 200 to 250 acres each. Only one young hedgerow is visible in the 1920 photograph below looking north from a point near the intersection of Horizon Reach and Ramsgate Road. Annapolis Road is seen at the right coming down from the hill.

From the 1840s, ranching activities were headquartered on both sides of the coast road about midway between Black Point and the Gualala River. Livestock were pastured around the Knipp Stengel Barn, and the ranch foreman resided on the hill above where they could keep an eye on the cattle below. When Walter Frick acquired the property in 1916, he converted a cottage farther north on the coast road near Del Mar into his summer home. Frick took over the cottage that Hans Petersen, the Del Mar Mill foreman, had occupied. The cottage sat on the west side of the road between Del Mar Store and Del Mar School. Frick immediately gave the house a fresh coat of green paint and painted the trim white. Also freshened up was the fence that ran along the coast road on the edge of his property. In this photograph, dated between 1916 and 1920, the coast road is in the foreground. Behind the picket fence are the guest house on the right and the cottage house in the center.

Frick was a high-powered businessman who made a fortune when he was still a very young man. About 1910, he established a business partnership with Robert Burgess, owner of the 16,000-acre Diablo Ranch in Contra Costa County. Six years later, Burgess went bankrupt, and Frick bought the Diablo Ranch. That same year, he acquired title to the 5,000-acre Del Mar Ranch. Initially, he considered subdividing the ranch but then decided otherwise. His family loved the coast, even if Frick himself did not like the cold weather. Whenever he visited his Del Mar Ranch, Frick was on vacation. In this photograph from the early 1920s, Frick and an unidentified friend are sitting on a donkey who was dressed up with a bonnet and booties, perhaps for the annual Point Arena Fourth of July parade.

Walter Frick owned the Del Mar Ranch prior to his 1916 marriage to Helen Fay and the birth of their children. In the photograph above, taken in 1923, the Frick children posed for a photographer. Walter Jr. was five years old, Helen Jane was four years old, and Robert was six years old. The photograph below was taken about the same time in front of the cottage at Del Mar. From left to right are Walter Jr. and Helen Jane, who are seen riding dark horses, and Helen Fay, who stood by holding the reins for her son Robert. The American flag suggests that the photograph may have been taken around the Fourth of July.

Automobiles were still considered a rich man's toy when Walter Frick bought his 1913 black Pierce Arrow. He paid what was then considered an outrageous price of $4,300. That was about the same amount that many people used to purchase a home in a city. Frick could afford it, and he loved driving around with the convertible top down so he could be seen. Such a car spoke to the owner's wealth and taste. The climate near the Sonoma coast can be fierce during the winter and windy during the summer. Worse yet is the corrosive salty air that is kicked up as a spray from ocean waves. To protect his shiny black car, Frick had built a carriage barn. It stood until the late 1980s across Highway One from the Frick summer cottage at Del Mar. The carriage barn was located in the southeast corner of the intersection of Highway One and Deer Trail, just opposite the Del Mar School. The photograph at left was taken of Frick in his Pierce Arrow. The photograph below, taken in 1941, shows the carriage barn.

Coastal fog and winds make the ocean terraces suitable for grazing but limit the kinds of crops that can be successfully grown. Hay, apples, pears, potatoes, and peas have produced abundant yields, if cared for properly. Weather east of the coastal ridge is warmer, and the crops grow faster and ripen earlier. Hy McMillen grew apples and prunes on his orchard in Annapolis. He packed the fruit in sacks, which were then loaded onto his wagon. A team of six horses hauled McMillen's wagon to Bihler Landing where the sacks were loaded onto ships sailing to the Bay Area. The cold winds and fog along the coast were avoided by the native Pomo Indians, who only ventured to the coast to harvest sea foods but made their homes inland.

Thousands of Chinese men came to California to work the gold fields in the 1850s. When the tracks for the transcontinental railroad were being installed in the 1860s, the Chinese performed most of the heavy physical work. By 1870, when the federal census was compiled in Salt Point Township, there were hundreds of Chinese people living in the area. They comprised a significant portion of the population. Many lived in shacks along China Gulch, just south of Gualala. Hundreds worked for lumber companies and camped in the woods near the logging activities. Those who did not actually participate in the logging worked as cooks for the lumber crews. Many worked in private homes either as domestics or cooks. The Chinese were invariably single, young men without families whose bodies were shipped back to China after their deaths.

Six

TOO MANY SCHOOLS, TOO FEW SALOONS
1870s–1950s

As Annapolis Road passes through the eastern boundary of The Sea Ranch and approaches the Gualala River, there is a low, flat area known as Valley Crossing. This was a favorite place to hide liquor that had come in on freighters but which could not be immediately transported out of the area because of muddy roads. The spot was easily accessible to locals but more difficult for strangers to locate. During the early months of the 1920s, when bootleggers secretly sought hollowed-out stumps and dug shallow graves as hiding places for their liquor contraband, they were intently watched by children, who appeared to their teacher to be staring out the classroom window daydreaming. Locals claim that students who were attending school in Priscilla Cole's saloon alongside Annapolis Road knew more about stashed bootleg whiskey than the adults. The need to hide liquor until roads were dry enough to travel ended in 1926 when the coast road from Jenner to Gualala was completed.

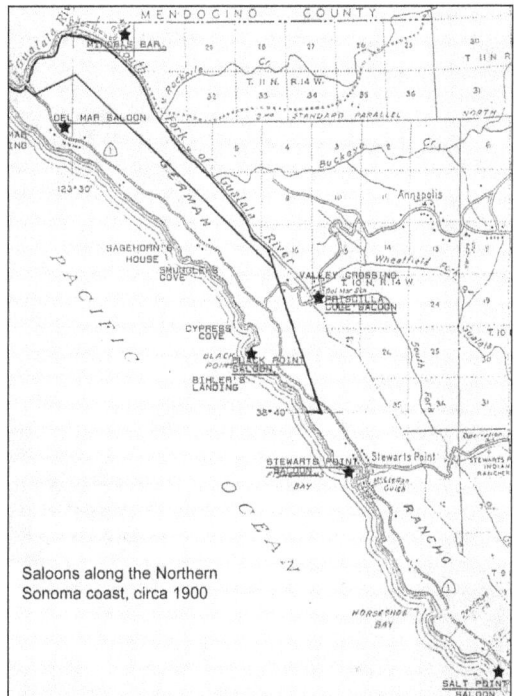

Saloons along the Northern Sonoma coast, circa 1900

John and Margaret Ohlson and their four sons—Edward, Chester, Ernest, and Elmer—lived 8 miles east of Stewarts Point. The boys attended Dirigo School in a little schoolhouse, which was established in the mid-1870s and was situated to the south of their home. In 1900, their teacher was Ima Herbert, a 20-year-old, unmarried woman from Iowa. She boarded with the Michael Williams family who lived next door to the school. This school photograph shows the students and teacher outside Dirigo School during the 1897–1898 school term. The Ohlson brothers transferred to Horicon School in Annapolis a few years after this photograph was taken. The students were identified by Ed Ohlson and are listed on the next page from left to right.

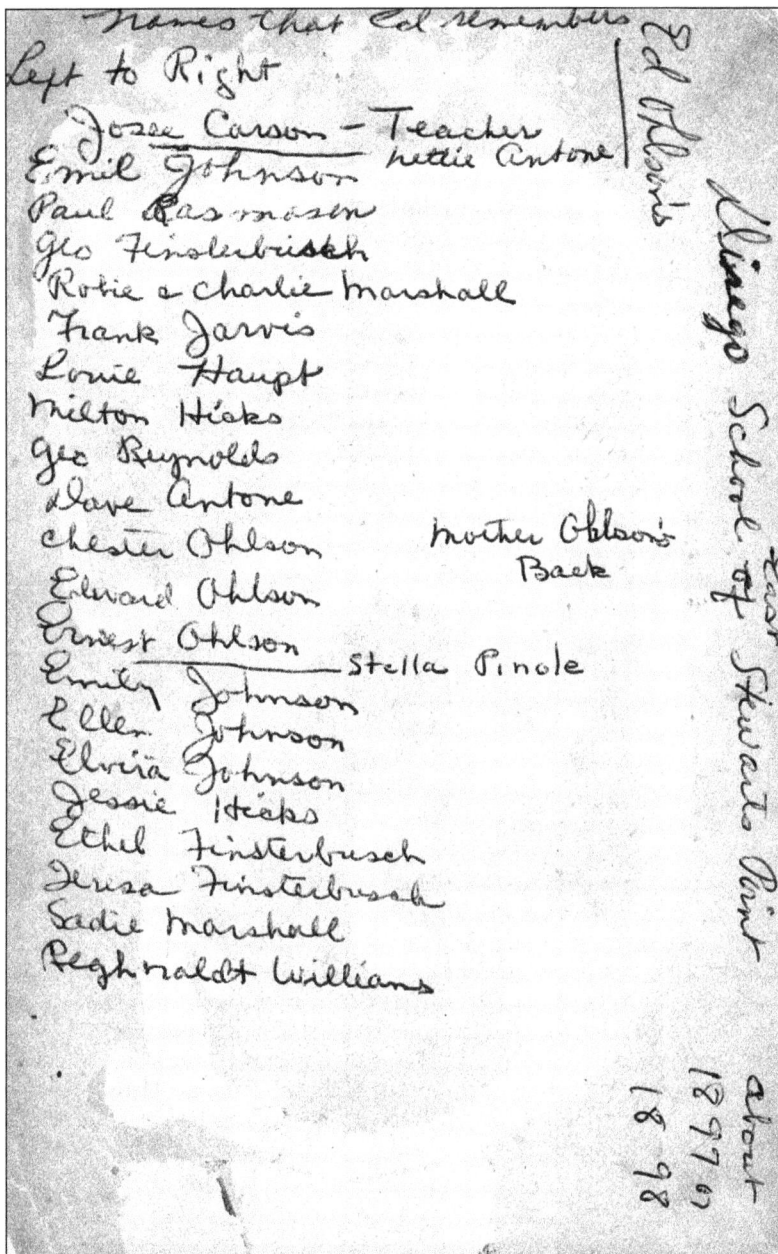

Names that Ed remembers

Left to Right

Josee Carson – Teacher
Emil Johnson   Nettie Antone
Paul Rasmusen
Geo Finsterbusch
Rotie & charlie Marshall
Frank Jarvis
Louie Haupt
Milton Hicks
Geo Reynolds
Dave Antone
Chester Ohlson   Mother Ohlson's
Edward Ohlson   Back
Ernest Ohlson
Emily Johnson _____ Stella Pinole
Ellen Johnson
Elvira Johnson
Jessie Hicks
Ethel Finsterbusch
Teresa Finsterbusch
Sadie Marshall
Reghnaldt Williams

Ed Ohlson's

Dirigo School of Stewarts Point

about 1897 & 98

Dirigo School was one of the earliest schools in Salt Point Township, constructed during the 1870s. The gable-roofed schoolhouse was a simple rectangle, with no cupola, bell tower, or gabled wings. It was located on Skyline Ridge, below Skaggs Springs Road and southeast of Clarks Crossing Bridge. The photograph on the previous page was taken during the 1897–1898 school term when there were more than 20 students. Ed Ohlson, who appears in the photograph, listed the names of the students he remembered—Johnson, Rasmussen, Jarvis, Finsterbrush, Marshall, Haupt, Hicks, Reynolds, Antone, Ohlson, Pinole, and Williams. The teacher was Josee Carson. As other schools were constructed and the demographics in the area shifted, attendance at Dirigo declined. During the 1917–1918 school year, when Ethyl Burnnight was the teacher, attendance had fallen to five students.

At the end of the 19th century, many one-room schools were built if there were at least eight children in the area. Many of the earliest schools dating from the 1870s were a simple rectangle with a gable roof. By the end of the century, schools like that at Stewarts Point, shown above, and Horicon School in Annapolis had gabled wings, which enclosed anterooms, and even a cupola. There was always an outhouse behind or to the side of the schoolhouse. Here are two photographs taken of the inside of the Stewarts Point School. The classroom had a piano, wood stove, and even curtains in the windows. Classes were held in the school until the late 1950s.

Horicon School in Annapolis originally stood on the Wetmore property. In June 1887, H. A. Richardson was paid $79 to move it to its present location. Relocating buildings was far more common at that time than it is today. The photograph above dates from 1902 and shows many of the same children who appear in the photograph of Dirigo School on page 76. The porch and cupola were added later, as can be seen at right. The school was also rotated, which accounts for the steps in the photograph at right.

RECORD OF ATTENDANCE

First Month, from _____ Dec. 2, 1912 to Dec. 28, 1912 _____
(Name and date of.)

Elisabeth E. Briggs Teacher

NAMES OF PUPILS.	Age of Pupil	Grade
1. Aleroff John	9	A1
2. Bramantoff Paul	10	B2
3. Bramantoff Violet	8	A2
4. Ermakoff Victor	6	A1
5. Hopin Anna	6	A1
6. Kunakov Dunia	11	A3
7. Kunakov Peter	13	B3
8. Lukianov Anna	13	B2
9. Lukianov Olga	7	A1
10. Lukianov Tania	11	B1
11. Noshkin Alexander	12	A1
12. Noshkin Katherine	13	A1
13. Noshkin Nadia	11	A1
14. Noshkin Love	7	A1
15. Noshkin Vera	10	A1
16. Noshkin Victor	6	A1
17. Panamoroff Mary	10	B1
18. Panamaroff Nicki	12	A3
19. Podsekiov Nicholas	7	A1
20. Podsekiov Willie	8	A1
21. Rodin Mania	11	A2
22. Gubachoff Michael	14	A4
23. Gubachoff Nastia	6	A1

Number enrolled _____ 23
Average daily attendance _____ 22

The schoolhouse at Del Mar had already been converted to a residence by 1912 when the Russian colonists settled on the Del Mar ranch. When the colonists requested Sonoma County provide them with a school and teacher, the county sent Russian-speaking Elizabeth Briggs to teach the students and arranged to have classes conducted in the old Del Mar saloon. After the mill at Del Mar burned in 1910 and the mill workers moved away to other jobs, there were not enough patrons to keep the saloon in business. The old saloon, which was renamed Sacel School, sat north of the present Del Mar meeting hall and east of the county road. The students' ages ranged from 6 years to 14 years old. A photograph of the saloon/school has not been located, but the attendance record provides valuable information about the names and ages of the students. With an average attendance of 22, Sacel School boasted more students than most other schools in the area. Sonoma County maintained Sacel School until the mid-1920s, when attendance dropped to only six students.

GENERAL RECORD

HER'S OPINION AS TO WHERE PUPIL SHOULD IN WORK UPON THE REOPENING OF SCHOOL.	NAME OF PARENT	RESIDENCE
	1 Theodore Aleziff	Del Mar.
	2 William Podushow	Del Mar
	3 Theodore Aleziff	Del Mar.
	4	
	4 Savely Hunahov	Del Mar.
	5 Mitrofan F. Kuznitzoff	Del Mar
	6 M. F. Kuznitzoff	Del Mar.
	7 M. F. Kuznitzoff	Del Mar.
	8 M. F. Kuznitzoff	Del Mar
A Fourth.	9 M. F. Kuznitzoff	Del Mar.
	10 Mitrofan F. Kuznitzoff	Del Mar.
	11 Timothy S. Korneyer	Del Mar.
	12 Finagay J. Lukianov	Del Mar.
	13 Finagay J. Lukianov	Del Mar.
	14 Finagay J. Lukianov	Del Mar.
	15 Emilian F. Noshkin	Del Mar.
	16 E. F. Noshkin	Del Mar.
	17 E. F. Noshkin	Del Mar.
	18 E. F. Noshkin	Del Mar.
	19 E. F. Noshkin	Del Mar.
	20 Emilian F. Noshkin	Del Mar.
	21 S. Rodin	Del Mar
	22 M. F. Kuznitzoff	Del Mar.
	23 John Ayermakov	Del Mar.
B. Sixth.	24 George P. Panamaroff	

Sonoma County School Board converted the old Del Mar Saloon to a schoolhouse, which opened for classes the first week in December 1912. Twenty-three children attended classes during the day and 13 parents attended at night. Every one of the children and their parents were born in Russia. Seen here is the list made by teacher Elizabeth Briggs of the grade each student should start when school resumed and the students' parents' names. Elizabeth Briggs also maintained a sign-in record for visitors to the school with the date of the visit. The visitors' record shows that people outside of the Russian community were interested in the Russian students. Beginning December 2, 1912, and continuing until school closed in 1913, visitors arrived from Los Angeles, Gualala, Point Arena, San Francisco, and Annapolis. The Russian colonists resided on the coast just a little more than one year, but the school records that remain are detailed and provide insight into the curriculum, students' ages, parents, and visitors.

After the Bender Brothers mill burned at Del Mar, the lumbermen and their families moved farther inland. About 1912, Sonoma County moved the location of Del Mar School to a small building that had served until recently as a saloon owned and operated by Priscilla Cole. Although national Prohibition did not become law for several more years, the Temperance Movement was very popular in California. Public sentiment blamed drinking for many of society's ills. Many saloons, like Cole's near Valley Crossing, closed. This photograph, dated 1920, shows the teacher with students outside the saloon, which had been adapted for school purposes. The school sat on the north side of Annapolis Road, and students had a full view of the smuggling activities that passed by the school. When a mother ship with liquor from Canada or Mexico anchored offshore, tenders brought the cargo to secluded beaches where it was transferred to car, trucks, and horse-drawn wagons. Shipments were delivered to Annapolis packed on wagons and covered with layers of apples to disguise the contents. If the wagon was noticed by law enforcement, no one seemed to question why apples grown in Annapolis were being hauled to Annapolis.

During the 1920s, freighters, called mother ships, from British Columbia came down the coast loaded with whiskey. The freighter stayed in international waters, and small launches brought the illegal cargo to shore. One of the most frequently used places for unloading was Smugglers Cove, where the water was deep, about a mile south of the Knipp Stengel Barn. Another choice place was near Black Point—named "Cypress Cove" by the bootleggers because of the Monterey cypress hedgerow nearby. After dark, the contraband was loaded onto waiting wagons or trucks parked near the shore, which would keep their headlights off as they turned around and headed off. Twelve gates, like cattle guards, crossed the coast road as the road passed through the Del Mar Ranch. A lawman hoping to catch bootleggers red-handed was at a disadvantage. As he approached the potential crime scene, opening and closing the 12 gates, his headlights cast a beam through the night darkness. His approach was seen by a lookout who alerted his comrades on the shore, so they had time to escape with the cargo or stash it in Black Point Barn.

During the mid-1920s, a new Del Mar School was built on the south side of Annapolis Road behind the current Sea Ranch Association office. It burned within a couple of years, and the school moved back into Priscilla Cole's saloon. This photograph dates from the mid-1930s, when Stella Von Arx was the teacher. Two of Priscilla's grandsons, Art and Tom Christensen, were students at the school at the time of this photograph. The eucalyptus tree in the background is still standing. The saloon/school burned in the 1970s.

Before 1910, a little cabin was built partway up the hill between the Knipp Stengel Barn and the eucalyptus crown. The schoolteacher lived there. Teachers in the area usually made between $65 and $75 per month. Generally, they were single, young women because it was expected that married women would stay home and take care of their husband and children. Most of the young teachers boarded with a family whose children attended the school.

Seven

THE OHLSONS AND THE
WAR YEARS
1941–1964

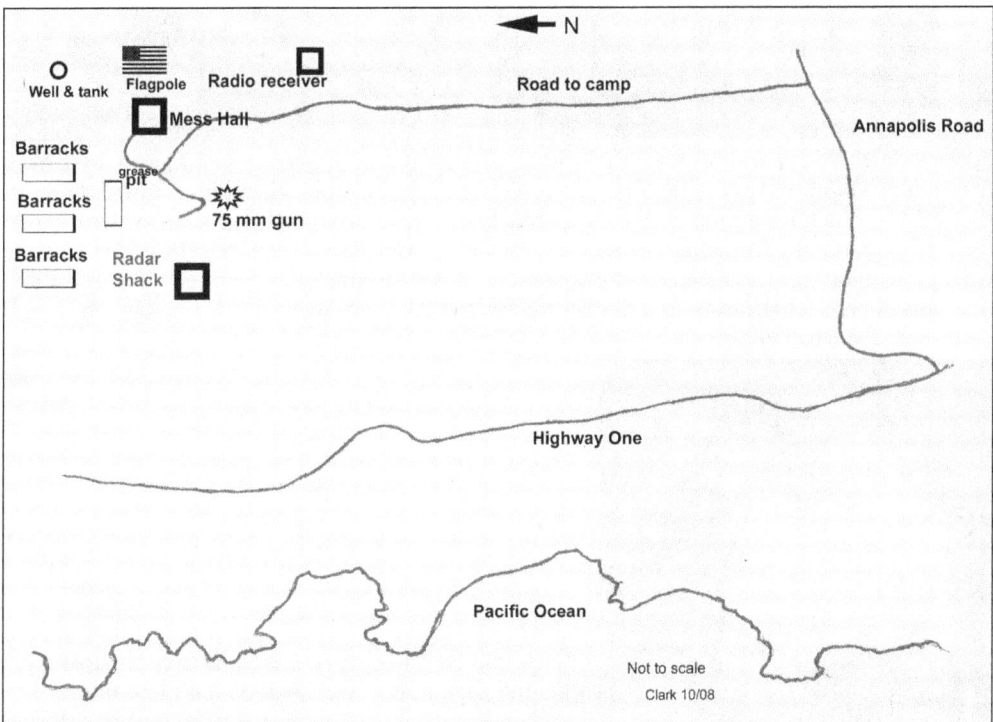

During the years that followed the bombing of Pearl Harbor, the U.S. government established dozens of small signal corps camps along the coasts of California, Oregon, and Washington. The purpose of these camps was to be on the lookout for any enemy activity along the coastal strip. In 1942, a small military camp was constructed on the edge of the timberline about three-fourths of a mile north of Annapolis Road and less than a half mile above the highway. The most identifying characteristic of the group of buildings was that it was designed to look like a cluster of sheep sheds. In 1942, about 100–200 men and several dogs moved into the camp. Roy Disotelle, later a restaurateur in Point Arena, was assigned as the cook for the station on Del Mar during the war. He provided the information on the sketch shown in this photograph. The camp was located near the intersection of Timber Ridge Road and Drovers Close. It spread southwesterly from the Drovers Close cul-de-sac.

Edward (Ed) Ohlson and his younger brother Chester (Ches) moved to Del Mar in 1941 from their family's farm in Annapolis. They along with their youngest brother, Elmer, raised sheep on the Del Mar ranch from then until they retired. Ernie, the fourth brother, continued farming on the Ohlson ranch in Annapolis. After they bought the Del Mar Ranch in 1941, Ed became the business manager for the sheep-raising operation. Elmer was the foreman. Sheep were separated into fenced pens for shearing and marketing. Ed and Ches are seen in this photograph, which dates from the late 1940s or early 1950s.

Ches and Ed Ohlson pried abalone from the rocks behind their home. The abalone was plentiful and grew to be much larger, as can be seen in this photograph taken during the late 1950s or early 1960s. Once The Sea Ranch was developed beginning in the mid-1960s, Sea Ranchers began to fish for abalone but put tight limits on how many they could take. They claimed responsibility for protecting the environment and native wildlife. After the Coastal Act was passed in 1972, public access ways through The Sea Ranch were opened in the 1980s. In just 20 years, public access has led to the irresponsible stripping of abalone from most of the offshore rocks. Abalones the size of those seen in the photograph are rarely seen today.

The Ohlsons were living in the cottage near Del Mar when these photographs were taken in the early 1940s. The south and east elevations are seen above. The rear or west elevation is seen below. The board and batten siding was stained green. The house was made up of three small buildings, which were constructed during the 1860s and 1870s. They had been originally located between the coast at Del Mar and the coast road. Soon after 1900, they were relocated and moved together to form one house. In one of the buildings, a brick with the date 1861 was discovered. Ed's wife, Alice, told neighbors she would often twist her ankle where the floor level changed heights. To the south of the house was a guest house, which was removed when the Ohlsons built a new home in 1951.

Before 1921, Frick had two overseers: Albert Ball, who lived above the Knipp Stengel Barn in the Stengel house near the eucalyptus crown, and Michael Williams, who lived in a small, two-story house where the road entering the North Recreation Center is today. When Fred Sagehorn was hired as ranch foreman, Frick had a new house constructed for him. The new house, seen in this photograph, stood between the current Ohlson Ranch Center and the coast highway. It was to this new house that Fred and his wife brought home their first and only child, David, born in 1922.

During the 1920s, Frick made several expensive investments in the Del Mar Ranch. Besides upgrades to the Cottage House, replacing fencing along the highway, and having a new house built for the foreman, he had a long structure constructed just south of the Knipp Stengel Barn in which farm vehicles and equipment could be stored. The equipment building, seen in this 1941 photograph, is still standing today. To lessen the damage the salty air would cause on the equipment, Frick had the openings on the building open to the east and had doors installed to provide additional protection from the harsh weather.

The Knipp Stengel Barn was almost 60 years old when the Ohlsons took over the Del Mar Ranch. Coastal storms, which often come from the south, had clearly weathered the south-facing elevation. The center opening in the south end was smaller than it is today. The sliding door was mounted on the interior of the wall, rather than on the exterior as it is today. The west and south elevations are seen in the photograph above. The photograph below shows the east and south elevations. It is interesting to note that there is only one row of "windows" on the east elevation and that the north elevation did not have a center door but had narrow passage doors with ramps at each end.

The structures in the two photographs on this page resemble one another, but they served two very different functions during the Frick and Ohlson years. The image above shows a water-tank shed that sat on the rise above Ed Ohlson's house, now the Del Mar Center. The nearby spring fed the water tank, which was housed in this small building. Water from the tank was gravity fed to the Ohlson residence. The photograph below shows one of many similar sheepherder cabins that were scattered about the ranch. When one of the ewes or young lambs needed special attention, a man would stay in the cabin and tend to the ewe or lamb, which was kept in the fenced area attached to the rear of the cabin.

Violent storms with high winds and waves are frequent visitors to the Sonoma coast. Tornadoes have been reported very infrequently. Recently (2005), one of the Pedotti barns at the Jenner Grade was destroyed by a tornado, but the other buildings were spared. The two photographs from Ed Ohlson are of damages from a 1950 tornado at the north end of the Ohlson ranch near the Gualala River mouth. As seen in the photographs, the path of the tornado swept across the north end and bent or broke several tall trees. It tore through one building, completely, but it left a nearby fence.

U.S. military activities intruded on the daily lives of the Ohlson family. Even before December 1941, when America declared war on Japan, the United States sent blimps along the coast to detect any foreign submarines. This photograph, dated 1941, shows a blimp over the cottage. Pat (Ohlson) Ashurst remembers an American pilot crashing nearby. No one was sure if the pilot had parachuted and survived or crashed. Hundreds of men combed the hills and beaches looking for any trace of the pilot. When a piece of fabric with the pilot's name was found on the beach, the pilot was presumed to have crashed at sea. The pilot's parents arrived from South Dakota and stayed with the Ohlsons for several days. For many years, they continued to send flowers to be tossed in the ocean on the anniversary of their son's death.

In 1941, the grasses were high, and it was a good year for raising sheep on the coast. The United States knew war was right around the corner, so the prices for lamb and wool were high. For several years there were even subsidies for sheep raisers. A good shearer could shear 140–180 sheep per day. The fleece was tied before being stuffed in a sack. The sacks were then loaded onto a truck and hauled away.

In 1941, Pat Ohlson and her brother Russ were 9 years old and 5 years old, respectfully, when their father and his brothers bought the Del Mar Ranch at auction on the steps of the Contra Costa Courthouse in Martinez. Walter Frick had died in 1937, and his coastal ranch was being sold by the sheriff for unpaid property taxes. Pat and Russ were the first children to grow up on the ranch from the time it was first settled in the 1840s. In this 1940s photograph, Russ and Pat pose with their dog in front of the 1930s rock wall that was built between the cottage house and the highway. The image below shows Russ and Pat on horses near the Knipp Stengel Barn. The eucalyptus crown above the barn is seen behind them.

There was little local entertainment that was of interest to the 20-year-old soldiers. When they got a day off, they tried to hitch a ride into Santa Rosa or Healdsburg. Sometimes a movie was shown in the mess hall, but usually the men had to make their own entertainment. On movie nights, the men would invite the Ohlson family to join them to share the movie. Mary and Alice Ohlson, wives of Ernest and Ed, occasionally visited the camp and entertained the men by playing the piano and singing. Here the women are seen arriving at the camp. Christine Reemus is at the far left, Alice Ohlson second from right, and Pat Ohlson at the far right.

This photograph represents a little-known period of Sea Ranch history. Until 1982, when locals who had lived in the area all their lives were asked about the old concrete or indentations in the ground that were around the intersection of Timber Ridge Road and Drovers Close, they responded with a blank stare. In about 1982, inquiry was made of Harold Christensen, who had been born a mile or so from the spot and who had lived all his 83 years in the area. He did not hesitate a minute as he recalled that a military camp had been located there during World War II. The water tank and flagpole were located on the high (east) side of Timber Ridge. Harold said most water used on the Del Mar Ranch came from springs. The well above Drovers Close was either the first, or one of the first, successful wells. It served the needs of the 150–200 men who lived on the hill during the war.

This is one of several barracks, built to house between 30 and 50 men each. The wooden-floor barracks were heated with oil burners, so fireplaces would not be necessary for heat. The officers headed by 2nd Lt. Lloyd Winslow had their separate quarters. The facility was known as Army Airbase Unit 463. When the unit first arrived, it reported to Hamilton Field in Marin County. Later it reported to an underground facility at Grizzly Peak in the hills outside Berkeley. The unit's call numbers were "George Dog 6." Others in the area were Jenner, "George Dog 5," and Fort Bragg, "George Dog 7." The base was established in 1942 and was dismantled in 1946. During the war, the navy used the present golf course area for bombing practice. The U.S. Coast Guard patrolled the beaches at night for any suspicious activity.

Some of the broken concrete, which is still alongside Timber Ridge Road, is from the floor of the recreation hall. It sat on a concrete-slab floor and served as a combination recreation hall, post office, mess hall, and shower room. A sheep fence, which encircled the recreation hall, contributed to its disguise as a farm building. Recreational offerings were sparse, so if men got a night off they usually went into Santa Rosa, Gualala, or visited the Ohlson family. A glimpse of the interior of the recreation hall with a pool table and a sign for the post office is seen in the photograph at right. The low gable-roof building below was the camp's bath/toilet house. Some of the camp's 35 dogs are also in the picture. The building materials and the style and placement of the windows suggest that they were recycled from another structure. Of course this building also contributes to the appearance of the camp as a farm complex.

Roy Disotelle, who later owned Disotelle's restaurant in Point Arena, grew up in New York before being drafted during World War II. Disotelle was cook at the air base and then stayed on after the war and married Marie Biaggi. His photographs, which are included in this book, are the only known photographs of Army Airbase Unit 463. For 50 years after the war ended, the military denied any knowledge of the base on the Del Mar Ranch. Then one day in the mid-1990s, some members of the Army Corps of Engineers arrived at The Sea Ranch and wanted to be taken to the site of the air base. Disotelle and the barracks are shown in both photographs. The windows seen below are covered so aircraft passing overhead at night would not catch glimpse of any light coming from the barracks.

The air base soldiers had time to enjoy themselves. A group of the men are seen at right in front of the Gualala Hotel in 1943. The photograph below shows Roy Disotelle and Marie Biaggi (couple at right, with two other couples). Sometimes men found trouble when they had some time off. One story is told of a night when a soldier drove a truck filled with other soldiers into Santa Rosa. Upon their arrival, the driver announced the time and place where they should meet for their ride home. When the evening was over, all the men except one had arrived back at the truck. The driver refused to wait for the latecomer and drove back up the coast. Hours later, when he was sound asleep, the driver was awakened by the man he left behind. The enraged man, who had hitchhiked and walked his way home, shot the driver as he lay in his cot.

The incendiary devices in the photograph were found on The Sea Ranch golf course in the 1980s. The metal devices usually measured between 8 inches and 10 inches and carried an explosive. They are remnants of Japanese military terrorist activities, which took place during World War II. During the war, Japanese attached incendiary devices to balloons that were launched from beaches in Japan into the prevailing winds. The balloons floated on air currents to the United States where the devices they carried were randomly dropped and exploded. Devoid of the sounds made by a ship or an airplane, the incendiary devices arrived and exploded without warning. Most balloons landed near the West Coast, but some floated as far inland as Iowa. In January 1945, the U.S. government restricted newspapers and radio news reports from disclosing any information regarding the devices, so that the Japanese would not know if the devices ever reached their target. Every few years, local newspapers continue to report the discovery of another incendiary device.

Alice Ohlson was known for her hospitality. Drop-in visitors were always welcome at the dinner table. The Ohlsons' nearest neighbors to the south were the Richardsons at Stewarts Point, and to the north the closest residents were in Gualala across the county line. The family retained close connections to the families they had known for a decade in Annapolis. Ernie, one of the four Ohlson brothers, still operated the family farm near Clarks Crossing. Impassable roads often made it difficult or downright impossible for high school students living in the outlying areas of Annapolis to get to Point Arena High School. Sometimes students would board with the Ohlsons during the week and return to home in Annapolis for weekends. Alice Porter Fiscus, later the longtime Annapolis postmistress, boarded with the Ohlsons during her high school years. The Ohlson family and some of their coast friends posed by the rock wall located in front of their house when this photograph was taken.

The 7,000-ton Japanese freighter *Kenkoku Maru* was on her way to San Francisco to pick up a load of wheat when she got stuck in a cove near Black Point in April 1951. Rescue ships were immediately sent to pull the freighter back out to sea. Tugs and barges failed to move the ship. The effort went on for 25 days during which time the ship's hull was damaged even more by the constant beating of waves. The activity brought hundreds of people—rescue crews and spectators—to the area. Many camped at Black Point. It was great excitement for this quiet section of the coast. Finally on May 23, the *Kenkoku Maru* was rescued by the tug *Sea Prince* and towed to Todd Shipyard in Alameda where her hull was repaired, and she was sent to sea again.

Kenkoko Maru

4-28-51

#18

Everyone was friendly to the crew of the *Kenkoko Maru* during the 25 days it took to get the ship off the beach. Hull plates were patched from the inside. Compressed air forced the water out. Caterpillar-brand tractors were rigged on land to the ship to two 8-ton anchors placed offshore. With a large tugboat and a high tide, the *Kenkoko Maru* was finally pulled free with a whistle and a toot. The huge anchors were cut loose and still remain off Black Point Beach. Some of the smiling crew is seen below. The captain was depressed, and the crew prevented him from suicide, but reportedly he later did actually commit suicide. The ship was repaired and returned across the Pacific, but repairs later failed, and the ship sank in the Philippines.

—Staff Photo by John LeBaron

IT'S GOODBYE, not "au revoir," for men of the Kenkoku Maru. Bidding Stewarts Point a courteous, but firm farewell are (left to right): Suzuichi Morishita, quartermaster; Nobuo Kasahara, 2nd mate; Tsuyoshi Nishihashi, quartermaster; and Kyushiro Sakamoto, cook. Cook is wearing apron made of Japanese flour sack.

103

Two events took place in the early 1950s that made life easier for the Ohlsons. The first was the installation of electric wires along the coast. The second was the construction of a new home. The guesthouse was removed to make space for the new home, which was built just 1 foot away from their earlier home. The image above, dated February 1952, shows the cottage on the right and the new house immediately next to it on the left. The photograph below, also dated 1952, shows the new home, which was converted into the Del Mar Center in the mid-1990s.

Eight

GHOSTS OF SEA RANCH PAST
1964–2009

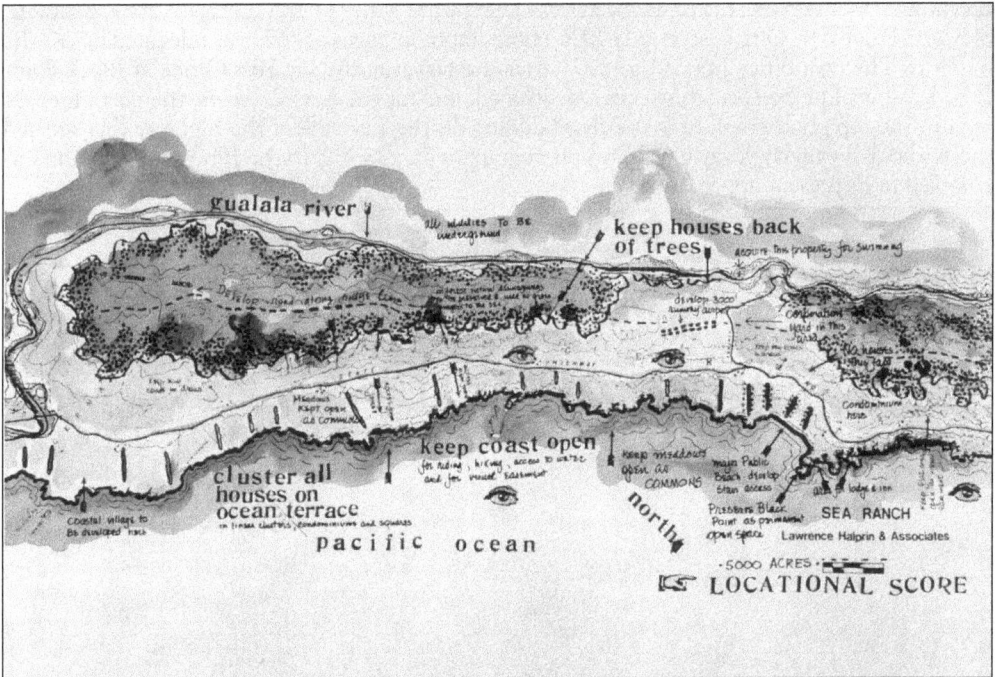

In 1963, Oceanic Properties, Inc., a subsidiary of Hawaii-based Castle and Cooke, was frustrated in its attempts to develop a planned community in Honolulu. Hawaii land-use legislation had frozen all development. Fred Simpich and Al Boeke, representatives of Oceanic Properties, Inc., flew to California in hopes of finding a suitable large tract of land to develop as a second home community. After seeing the Del Mar Ranch, they recommended that Castle and Cooke purchase the land. They hired master planners, including Lawrence Halprin, Charles Moore, and Donlyn Lyndon, to create a design scheme that blended into the environment. Halprin delved into all aspects of the environment—weather, land forms, hedgerows, water, soils, and beaches—before deciding on the basic premises shown here. The planners were inspired by the old barns and farm buildings on the ranch and developed the unique Sea Ranch style of architecture characterized by natural redwood and cedar exteriors and barnlike shed roofs.

Stewarts Point Post Office, seen in a 1926 photograph on pages 56–57, was relocated across the highway. The post office opened in 1903 after the Fisherman's Bay Post Office at Black Point closed. When The Sea Ranch was first developed, and for the next 20 years, the post office, as seen in the top photograph, was the first building on the east side of the highway that greeted those who drove up Highway One. This photograph is dated 1980. In the 1980s, the building was enlarged to its present appearance.

The Annapolis Post Office appearance has changed very little since Grace Fiscus became postmistress in 1903. She held the position until 1940 when she turned it over to her son Charley. Charley was postmaster until the late 1970s when his wife Alice took over.

Oceanic Properties, Inc., and subsequently The Sea Ranch Association preserved some of the old farm buildings for storage or simply to highlight the rural atmosphere of the ranch. New buildings at the Del Mar Center were designed with the barn shape, board and batten siding, and are painted white to resemble the adjacent white-washed farm buildings. The Del Mar Pool utilizes two old adjacent buildings as windbreaks for the pool area. The Ohlson residence was remodeled into small meeting rooms for committees and Sea Rancher usage. A new larger meeting hall was constructed next to the Ohlson house. The collection of white-painted buildings resembles or reflects the previous Ohlson farmstead.

Horseback riding was a recreational activity that Oceanic Properties, Inc., offered to Sea Ranch property owners. The Knipp Stengel Barn had an open interior that was easily adapted to a horse stable. Matt Silvia, a local contractor, constructed stalls, stable manager's office, a kitchen, a trophy room, and two bathrooms. A long horizontal window for the trophy room was installed in the north end. The northwest corner window was in the manager's office. One of the bathrooms blocked off the original north exit, so a new narrow stairway was installed just outside the corner bathroom. Twenty-three paddocks were developed on the meadow below the barn. A riding ring was fenced to the north of the barn. In the mid-1980s, Oceanic Properties, Inc., shut down the barn and the horses were kept outside in the paddocks. The number of horses dwindled until the Equestrian Facility was constructed on the opposite side of the highway.

After neglecting maintenance for several years, Oceanic Properties, Inc. transferred ownership of the Knipp Stengel Barn to The Sea Ranch Association. It was listed on the National Register of Historic Places in 1986. The association spent little money on stabilizing the building that was used for little other than storage. Safety and fire regulations prevented Sea Ranchers from using the building, with estimates of hundreds of thousands of dollars to make the barn reusable. In 1991, a group of volunteers, with the help of a few local contractors, took over the restoration and completely restored and upgraded the barn with a new foundation, new roof, new electrical and plumbing, and a sprinkler system. The labor was donated and became a weekly Saturday event. Many of the materials were also donated or purchased at reduced rates, thus saving the association many thousands of dollars. The barn is now used for large functions, including plays, celebrations, and meetings.

Initial construction by Oceanic Properties, Inc., began in 1965 with a Marker House at the corner of Sea Walk Drive, which was used as a post office and real estate office; the Sea Ranch Lodge; and the restaurant and store. This image was taken before 22 lodging units were constructed and Condominium I, consisting of 10 units, were built. Oceanic Properties, Inc., developed the Sea Ranch logo, which represents a ram's horn wrapped around a wave and a seashell. New paved roads followed many of the old farm roads. Residential parcels were created between the hedgerows, similar to Frick's concept of planting hedgerows to divide the ranch into "ranchettes." Sea Ranchers still use unit numbers when giving directions to their homes and often identify their location by their unit number. Annual parties are held in each unit where the only invitees are owners within that unit.

Condominium I was constructed just south of the Sea Ranch Lodge below Bihler Point. It majestically sweeps upward, near the plunging bluff that leads to the ocean. The architects, Charles Moore, Donlyn Lyndon, William Turnbull, and Richard Whitaker (MLTW), incorporated post and beam barnlike structural construction with open interiors, balconies, and skylights in a stacked cubic design. Bay windows command spectacular views along the coast. Service areas are tucked in corners and spaces around stairways. The sleeping area was a loft supported by four posts and enclosed by curtains for privacy. The 10 units surround a central parking/entrance court. The photograph above shows Condo I under construction and gives a feel for the adjacent steep bluff to the ocean. The Marker House can be seen in the background. The photograph below is taken from Bihler Point soon after construction was finished in the mid-1960s. Unit 10 has the three-story tower with a dramatic south coastal view. Condo I has attracted much attention, won many awards, and is known worldwide throughout the architectural community.

The Del Mar Store was located just north of the Del Mar Center on the west side of the highway. Bender Mill and Lumber Company built the store about the same time they constructed the lumber mill, 1897–1898, for the convenience of the mill workers and their families. When the mill was active, there were approximately 500 residents living at Del Mar. Then the mill burned in 1910, and the mill workers found work at other mills. There was a store in Gualala, located a couple miles to the north, and the population was too small to support a second store nearby. The store sat unused and deteriorating. In 1975, The Sea Ranch Association decided to document the building and then dismantle it. For several years, the building materials were stored for the unlikely possibility that eventually it would be rebuilt. But that time has passed. Fortunately, there were sketches made of the building plan, and the building was photograph-documented. The two pictures were taken in 1975, shortly before the store was taken down.

By the 1970s, the Sea Ranch Lodge, shown in the photograph, had been expanded into a larger restaurant, post office, store, real estate office, and adjacent 22 lodging units. Thousands of trees were planted, which in recent years add to fire danger and require management. Over 1,800 lots had been sold and over 500 houses of the planned 5,000 houses had been built. The environmental movement pushed for protecting the coast and shutting down development along the California coast. The Sea Ranch was targeted as a massive development and was shut down in 1976 by the newly formed California Coastal Commission. A 5-year legal fight was finally settled in 1981 by the Bane Bill. The Sea Ranch was restricted to a maximum of 2,329 lots, and five public accesses were granted to allow the public access to the coast beaches.

GHOSTS OF THE PAST

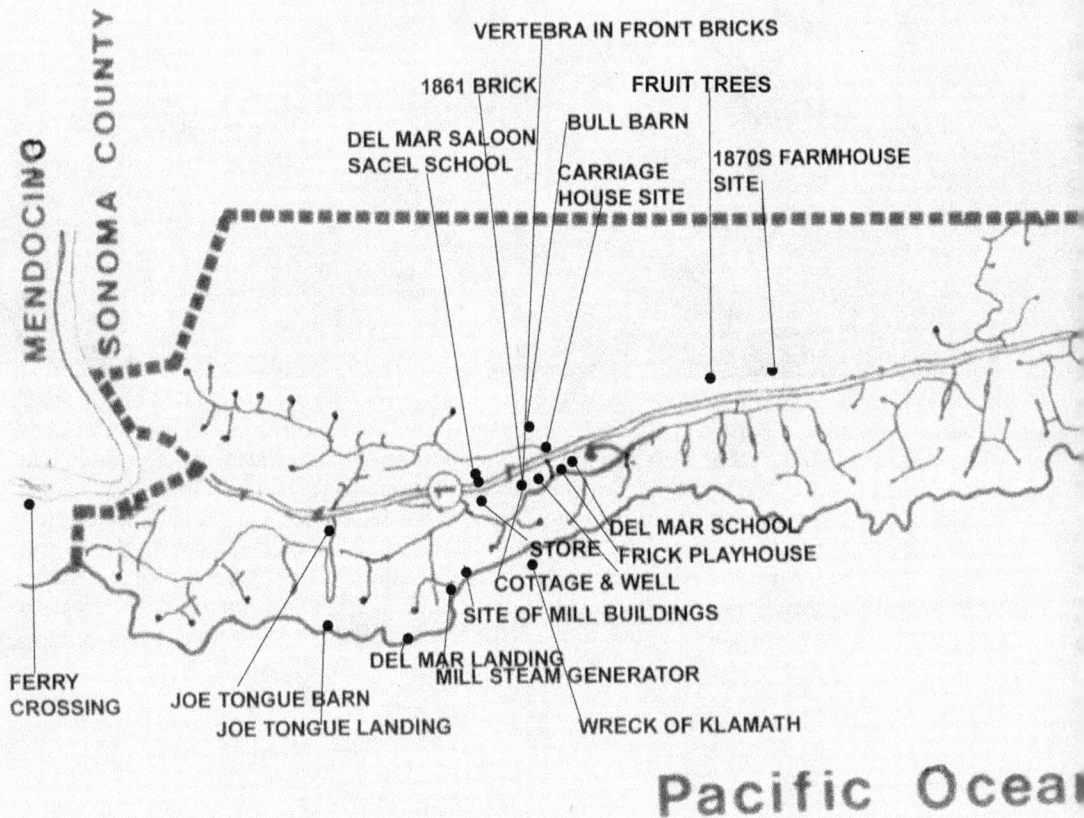

VERTEBRA IN FRONT BRICKS

1861 BRICK   FRUIT TREES

BULL BARN

DEL MAR SALOON
SACEL SCHOOL   CARRIAGE   1870S FARMHOUSE
                    HOUSE SITE   SITE

MENDOCINO

SONOMA COUNTY

DEL MAR SCHOOL
STORE   FRICK PLAYHOUSE
COTTAGE & WELL
SITE OF MILL BUILDINGS

DEL MAR LANDING
MILL STEAM GENERATOR

FERRY
CROSSING   JOE TONGUE BARN
        JOE TONGUE LANDING   WRECK OF KLAMATH

Pacific Ocea

Images of some well-known and lesser-known historic sites and artifacts are shown in chapter eight. The map pictured above identifies some of their locations to entice Sea Ranchers and

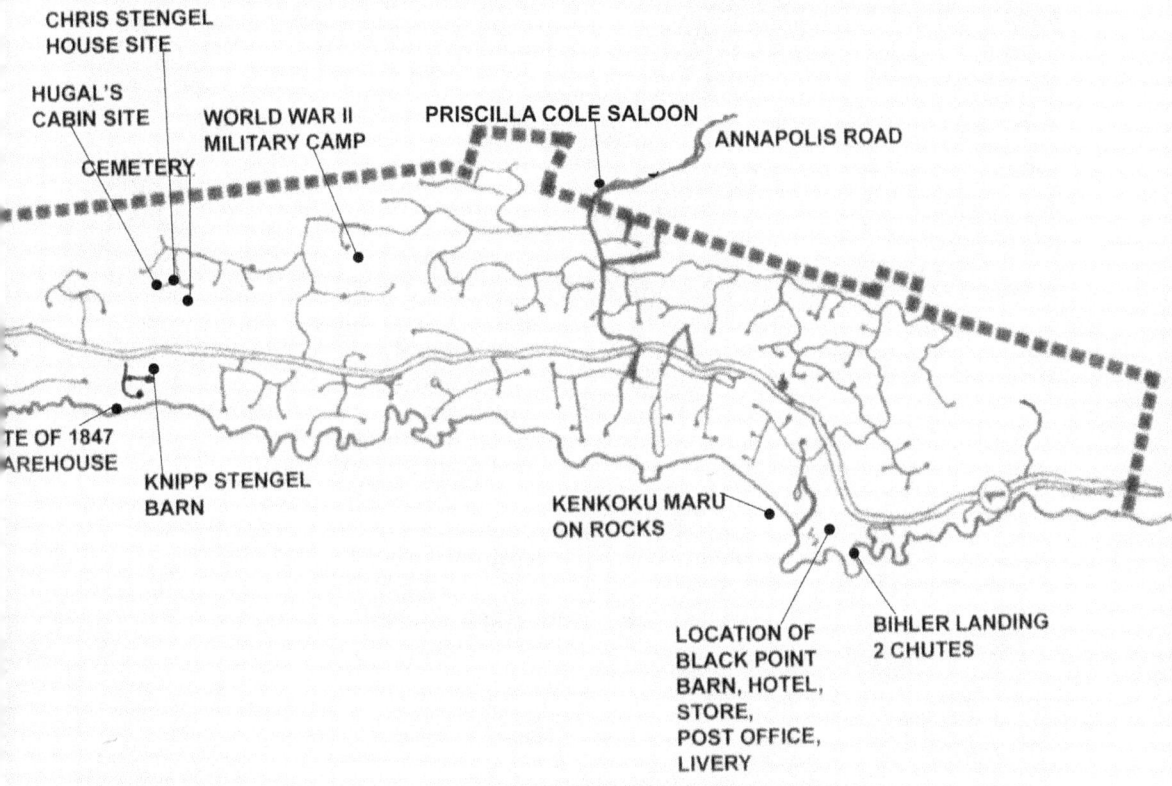

CHRIS STENGEL
HOUSE SITE

HUGAL'S
CABIN SITE

CEMETERY

WORLD WAR II
MILITARY CAMP

PRISCILLA COLE SALOON

ANNAPOLIS ROAD

TE OF 1847
AREHOUSE

KNIPP STENGEL
BARN

KENKOKU MARU
ON ROCKS

LOCATION OF
BLACK POINT
BARN, HOTEL,
STORE,
POST OFFICE,
LIVERY

BIHLER LANDING
2 CHUTES

visitors to explore and enjoy the history of The Sea Ranch.

The construction of the mill at Del Mar in 1897 brought many new families to the area around the mill. At that time, the closest school was on the North Fork of the Gualala River. The operators of the mill constructed a new schoolhouse for the children in 1905, and the desks and supplies were brought from North Fork School to Del Mar. The 16-by-20 foot, one-room school was built of redwood and served as a school for only seven years. After the Del Mar Mill burned in 1910, the number of students dwindled as families relocated north or to Annapolis. For the next 50 years, the building served as living quarters for ranch hands and sheepshearers. The image above dates from 1982 when the schoolhouse was neglected and open to the weather. Beginning in 1983, Sea Ranch volunteers undertook the challenge of repairing the building and giving it a new roof and foundation. The schoolhouse, seen in the 2008 photograph below, and the Frick playhouse, which sits just to the north, are highly visible reminders of the past.

The last two remaining fruit trees from an orchard planted in the 1880s by Cyrus Robinson of Gualala still stand east of the highway from Leeward Spur. Robinson, owner of Gualala House and later Gualala Hotel, owned a 100-acre tract, which included Unit 28 and the land adjoining the land to the east of the highway. There are some red bricks remaining from a house that was located south of the orchard. Early maps show several buildings in that area above the highway and cultivated fields on the meadows that make up today's Unit 28. The two trees currently produce fruit that seems to be a cross between an apple and a pear. Their abundant fruit is enjoyed by the deer and other animals. The photograph below was taken by Sea Rancher Bob Marshall.

Black Point Barn is the only remaining building from the group of structures dating from the late-1870s development of Bihler's Landing. It originally served as the livery stable for the hotel. When Bihler's Landing closed in 1902, people moved away from the area and the barn was no longer used. During the Russian colonists' occupation of the Del Mar Ranch in 1912–1913, they scavenged wood from the buildings at Black Point Barn to fuel their steam tractors. By 1920, there were only 4 of the original 13 buildings still standing. During Prohibition, rumrunners often unloaded their illegal cargo onshore and stashed it in Black Point Barn until they could move it after dark. After Castle and Cooke, Inc., developed the Sea Ranch Lodge in 1965, the barn deteriorated until the 1980s when it was restored. It now offers a venue for weddings and other celebrations. The photograph above was taken before restoration; the image below shows its current appearance.

The photograph of Nicholas Podsakoff's grave (also on page 63) was taken early in the 20th century. Ed Ohlson had lived in the nearby house at Del Mar since 1941 and was very familiar with the circle of stones marking the grave. In 1977, he was shown the old photograph and attempted to locate the stones by walking along the bluff edge between Del Mar Point and Sea Stack. He finally decided that the stones had remained uncovered as long as there were sheep to eat down the grasses. The sheep were removed in 1965 when the Ohlsons sold the ranch and then the sod grew up, covering the stones. On a very rainy day in 1982, a few Sea Ranchers searched for the offshore rocks seen in the photograph near the area Ohlson had identified. When the rocks offshore resembled those shown in the photograph, a long stick was poked in the soggy earth to feel for the stones. There they were on a straight line from Sea Stack, about 2 feet from the bluff edge. The photograph dates from 1982.

The only remaining bull barn is in ruins near the southeast corner of Highway One and Deer Trail. It sits on the north side of a ravine well below the level of the highway. During the late 19th and early 20th centuries, teams of oxen were used to pull freshly cut logs from the woods down to the mill at Del Mar or to a connection point with a spur rail line that would take the logs the rest of the way to the mill. At the end of the day, the oxen were taken to the barn where they were fed and stabled overnight. Bull barns were frequently located at the edge of the timberline, out of the wind, and partway between the mill and the woods. Another bull barn was located on the high side of the unpaved road that leads into the walk-in cabins.

Helen Fay and Walter Frick's only daughter, Helen Jane, was born in 1919. In the early 1920s, Frick had a playhouse built behind the summer cottage for Helen Jane. It was board and batten and had a gable roof and windows that opened and closed. On the west side of the playhouse, he planted an apple tree. The playhouse sat alongside Leeward Road on a strip of commons between Heron and South Wind. During the 1980s, the small building was deteriorated (below) and beginning to fall apart. Bushes and weeds grew up around it and hid it from the view of passersby on Leeward Road. In the early 1990s, the playhouse was picked up and relocated to the north of Del Mar School, near the corner of Leeward Road and Deer Trail. Its siding has been repaired, and it has been reroofed. The apple tree planted by the playhouse still marks its original location and bears shiny green apples today.

The rock-walled well sits in the garden to the south of the Del Mar Center. It was overgrown with bushes and weeds when Oceanic Properties, Inc., acquired the Ed Ohlson house in the mid-1980s. The well was used by the Ohlsons and the Fricks before them. When the Coast and Geodetic Survey of the coast was made in late 1878 and early 1879, several buildings and a well were mapped between the coast road and the bluff. Three of those buildings were combined to make up the Frick summer cottage closer to the county road. It is possible that the well was relocated to the higher elevation at that time. The year-round creek, that comes from the east and empties at the shore southwest of the Del Mar Center, supplies the well.

Two of the oldest remnants of the past are located at Del Mar Center. When Ed Ohlson had his new home built in 1952, he brought from the Ohlson property in Annapolis a whale vertebra that was found on the family farm. It was mortared into the north side of the brick steps leading up to the front door. After Ohlson died in 1983, the house passed to Oceanic and then to The Sea Ranch Association. In 1996, when the property was converted into the Del Mar Center, the vertebra was left in place, where it is today. The 1861 brick seen below was mortared into the barbeque on the Ohlson back porch. It may have been discovered by the Ohlsons when their new house was under construction. Parts of the cottage dated from the 1860s. The barbeque was removed when the house was converted, but the brick was retained and sits in a niche above the west-facing fireplace.

Local residents who have shared remembrances of the years when Walter Frick owned the ranch always seem to mention Frick's Pierce Arrow car—even coastal residents who never met Frick but only heard of him from their parents mention the Pierce Arrow car. Clearly, automobiles were still relatively new along the northern Sonoma coast. And a Pierce Arrow, which cost $4,300 in 1913, was more unusual, yet. Only a few people are aware that Frick's Pierce Arrow is still on the coast. Archie (A. H.) Richardson, son of H. A. and Althea, bought the car for $700 in 1923. It has been restored (see above) by Archie's nephew Chet. The 1915 Stanley Steamer (seen below) was purchased new by H. A. Richardson's other son, Fontaine. Chet and Harold Richardson, Fontaine's son, are seen in a 2006 photograph of the car. It is still owned by the Richardson family.

In 1857, William Bihler sent to Baltimore for four of his nephews to help with his ranching operations in California. Whereas he assigned Adam Knipp and Chris Stengel to his property on the German Rancho, he assigned Jacob Stengel and Jacob Grengnagle to his property on the Huichica Rancho at the southern end of Sonoma and Napa Counties. On February 15, 1862, twenty-three-year-old Jacob Stengel died in a horse accident on Bihler's Napa County ranch. Word of his brother's death was sent to Chris. Jacob's body was transported from southern Napa County to northern Sonoma Country. Chris was living in a small cabin on a hill 5 miles from the Mendocino County line. He had a grave prepared for his brother close to his house on the hill. The tombstone is up the hill from the Knipp Stengel Barn.

No fewer than five people were buried on the hill above the Knipp Stengel Barn, beginning with Jacob Stengel in 1862. Jacob was the only burial associated with an owner of the property. The others were employees of the ranch or their relatives. When the Daughters of the American Revolution were transcribing Sonoma County tombstones in 1921, they recorded the grave of an infant daughter of Tom Hitchcock buried near the Stengel grave. Old-timers recall there being five headstones on the hill above the barn and to the south of the eucalyptus crown. Early Sea Ranchers claim to have seen two. The fence surrounding the grave was constructed by Oceanic Properties, Inc., to protect it when the lots on Rams Horn Reach were developed. Regardless, the fenced plot is a reminder of the people who lived and died on the Del Mar Ranch before anyone ever thought of The Sea Ranch.

INDEX

Visit us at
arcadiapublishing.com

· ·